1.   Bill Owens has been engaged to bring the Chinese and American militaries together for over a decade. I have supported and observed his work with great interest. He has a profound understanding of the Chinese and American systems and how they will play out at the decades ahead. I strongly recommend his work to those who care about the future of this most important relationship.
— Maurice R. Greenberg, Chairman & CEO, Starr Companies

2.   This timely and impressive book recognizes the enormous negative consequences for the United States, China and the world if the US and China choose a path of conflict rather than cooperation over the next 20 years.
— Richard Gephardt, Former Majority and Minority Leader, US House of Representatives, 1989-2003.

3.   Bill Owens has developed over many years, a trusted understanding of the Chinese and American militaries. He has done this through many dialogues with active duty and retired senior military officers. It's especially interesting that he has brought together a number of very thoughtful people to look at the next 20 years and then to provide broad policy recommendations to avoid potential conflict over those years and into the future. I strongly recommend this work.
— Tung Chee-hwa, Founder, China-US Exchange Foundation; Former Chief Executive of the Hong Kong Special Administrative Region

4. Bill Owens has contributed in many ways over the years to US China cooperation and friendship. This book is a must read for those who are serious about the subject of long-term partnership and friendship between the two great countries.

— Audie Wong, Executive Director, China-US Exchange Foundation; Former President. Amway China

5. "Having thought about the United States and China for decades, I strongly recommend this work. It is a serious contribution to bringing China and the United States back together …, much needed in our world today."

— Li Lu, Founder and Chairman, Himalaya Capital Management

China–US 2039: The Endgame?

Building Trust Over Future Decades

ADMIRAL BILL OWENS

This book is dedicated to the young adults of the United States and China who, in the next two decades, will shape the future of our countries and of the world.

December 2, 2019

China US 2039: The Endgame?
Admiral Bill Owens, retired

Are China and the United States destined for conflict or cooperation? *US-China 2039: The Endgame?* looks at the next two decades of China and America in a unique way and gives a view of "what it will be like then". Then the reader is given 12 concrete US Macro-Policy recommendations for those 20 years to avoid future conflict and confrontation, with the hope that a constructive relationship, possibly even partnership, could be developed between the world's two largest economies.

The rise of China, and how the United States responds to it in the coming decades, will be salient for not only the people in both countries but also the world at large. China's rise generates the specter of great power rivalry with the United States. The Chinese economy is providing the resources to develop military power to challenge the United States in the future and possibly to "win". The US Armed Forces are shifting force structure, creating new operational concepts, and developing weapons. The People's Liberation Army is doing the same creating a deadly spiral of instability as both militaries prepare for the worst.

Bill Owens, former Vice Chairman of the Joint Chiefs of Staff, has been advancing a constructive U.S-China relationship for decades. In this book, Owens combines his considerable military experiences, deep knowledge of the inner working of the national security apparatus, and insights from serving in leadership positions in numerous Fortune 500 companies, including serving as the CEO of a Fortune 100 company.

Following his retirement from the United States Navy in the 1996, where he served as Vice Chairman of the Joint Chiefs of Staff, Owens has worked tirelessly to bring together senior retired officers from the both China and the United States to discuss issues of critical concerns to both countries. These experiences and deliberations have informed the conclusions of this book. synthesizes the perspectives of practitioners in both countries, and *US-China 2039: The Endgame?* reflects much of the hundreds of hours of conversations which have taken place among these most senior military officers concerning these crucial challenges, and opportunities! Importantly, China thinks "long term", while the US does not! This book thinks in the next 20-year timeframe and provides specific policy recommendations oriented to that most critical time in US History. Jus a few of these recommendations follow:

- A Northeast Asia Consultative Permanent organization including China, the US, Russia, Japan, and South Korea focused on the issues of the Region
- A Free Trade Agreement between the US and China
- A No First Use of Cyber Agreement between the US and China

- A New Approach to the number one issue between the US and China: Taiwan
- Discussion and Recommendations about the never-before addressed new world issue of a "transparent large battlefield" realized by both China and the US and the resulting Mutual Assured Destruction which Must be avoided in that new world.
- Plus 7 other recommendations.

It is with the passion to improve the US-China relationship that this book was written, drawing on insights from numerous experts with decades of expertise. *US-China 2039: The Endgame?* will be a significant contribution to the ongoing debate on the U.S. approach to China.

TABLE OF CONTENTS

PREFACE

This book looks at the future of China and the United States. It's written from my heart, as I've watched China grow to what I believe will eventually be the world's largest economy. It will be a world in which my grandchildren will grow and live, and it is likely to be very different from my generation's world. The rise of China, and how the United States responds to it in the coming decades, will be salient for whether my grandchildren and their cohorts live well or not. China's rise generates the specter of great power rivalry with the United States. The Chinese economy is providing resources to develop the military potential to challenge the United States and possibly "win" in the future. In preparation for armed conflict, the United States Armed Forces are shifting force structure, operational concepts, and weapons. And the People's Liberation Army (PLA) is doing the same while focusing on a conflict with the United States.

The United States is emerging from our longest war, 17 years focused on terrorism, with the costs reaching roughly $6 trillion so far.[1] We cannot afford another one. What President Eisenhower labeled the *military-industrial complex* in 1961 cannot keep pace with such changes as the Pentagon continues to operate in the same way it did during the Cold War. We should invest significant resources in emerging technologies, space, cyber, and other areas that offer advanced capabilities, and we should develop them rapidly. This means we need new approaches to maintaining national security and must not permit any other nation to become militarily more powerful than the United States. That commitment will take far more than money, which will *not* be available given the current US deficit and a paucity of discretionary spending.

The perspective of the book is two decades ahead, extending to 2039. China thinks and plans for such swaths of time. But the US generally focuses on the shorter term, or roughly four years. Meanwhile, the Chinese are building long-term partnerships with dozens of nations through loans for infrastructure, shared technology, and joint ventures with the creators of telecom networks from Huawei Technologies to the ZTE Corporation. As the United States seems intent on dismembering its alliances and partnerships around the world, the Chinese are increasingly engaged with various countries in Europe, Southeast Asia, Africa, and Latin America, undertaken with long-term plans looking decades ahead.

I do not believe armed conflict between the United States and China is inevitable. However, many politicians, commentators, and military leaders think that it is increasingly likely. My perspective is influenced by my considerable military background, which includes serving as Vice Chairman of the Joint Chiefs of Staff, as well as by my subsequent business experience, which includes my role as Chief Executive Officer of a Fortune 500 company and senior membership on numerous international boards of corporations and international startups. From my vantage point, it is undeniable that the United States and China will be the two superpowers of 2039. The issue is whether we will be reaping the benefits of a constructive relationship or facing armed conflict for future decades. This book offers specific recommendations on how to avoid armed conflict, and instead create an alternative future in which both nations can prosper for the benefit of their citizens and the world.

In the last decade of the twentieth century, upon my retirement from the Navy and from my last assignment as Vice Chairman of the Joint Chiefs of Staff, I worked and lived in Hong Kong. One of my most interesting insights into what China was and is trying to do over the next 20 years has come from senior retired flag officers of the PLA. In 2009, together with American colleagues—all retired US four-star generals and admirals—I proposed Track II meetings[2] with our Chinese counterparts who retired after serving at an equivalent level in the PLA. We named these discussions the Sanya Initiative. Over the past decade, we have met once or twice each year for about four days in an informal setting, alternating between our two nations.

Our initial meetings a decade ago followed the polite rituals of diplomatic courtship and prepared talking points. But in more recent years, our discussions have moved away from prepared talking points designed to ensure military confidentiality and preserve security. They have become wide-ranging, open, and candid—largely because they are unofficial—covering a panorama of military experiences and views of one another's capabilities. We have engaged in thought experiments on the future of bilateral military affairs and security relationships. Over the past five years the meetings have generated some unexpected results and a rapport that has gone beyond our expectations among military men who collectively best understand the destructive potential of war, particularly in a nuclear age.

Our concluding dinners and meetings have included active-duty members from the Central Military Commission, and occasionally, members of the US Joint Chiefs of Staff, affording the opportunity for retired US flag officers to exchange ideas with senior Chinese active-duty officers. On many occasions, defense attachés from the American embassy in Beijing have joined us, providing them connections to the senior levels in the PLA. These kinds of discussions have actively contributed to avoiding and solving conflicts. Our meetings have built a level of trust that has enabled candid discussions on initiatives aimed at diverting our energies away from confrontation toward cooperation in pursuit of peaceful objectives, such as using PLA bases in the South China Sea for humanitarian missions, the possibility of Chinese logistics support in Afghanistan, and the North Korean situation. Moreover, the meetings have convinced the other American participants and me that it may be possible after years of building trust to hold discussions oriented toward a mutually supportive relationship between our two countries. I come away from the experience convinced we must build similar exchanges and networks in different fields. Of course, these are Track II discussions and clearly not official decision-making forums.[3]

I am convinced that the Chinese are seeking new solutions that could elicit both opportunities and challenges for the United States. From an American perspective, we must bear in mind that China will likely become a peer of the United States with an equivalent gross domestic product (GDP) and the potential to build a very competitive and advanced military within two decades. It is imperative that proposed initiatives start as soon as possible because their implementation will take time and diplomacy.

It has been almost two decades since I retired and turned to what I believe is the most important foreign and military policy area our nation faces over the next two decades: our relationship with China. It will be complicated and difficult to construct the coming world order that is beneficial to China, the United States, and the world (and the generations that will follow us). I think about it a great deal, and my understanding of what China seeks, based on my involvement since retiring from military service, is not radically different from that of many China experts and officials in the State and Defense Departments, at least regarding the next few years, which will focus on economic, military, and ideological competition between our two nations. But China and the United States can and should communicate openly and work together to avoid conflict and build ways to cooperate for the benefit of both Countries and the world around us. I offer two personal stories:

- When I visited the mayor of Chengdu and secretary of the Communist Party, the enduring memories of our wartime partnership and cooperation struck me. Both accompanied me on my visit to the immaculate Chinese-maintained memorial to the Americans who fought in China in World War II. It was a source of pride for both men, members of the Communist Party, who were too young to have remembered US military operations in China (which were largely in support of the Kuomintang). The mayor said he wished every American could understand the great friendship that once prevailed between the United States and China as an example for the future.

- Early in my career with the United States Navy I served in the Vietnam War, as did many others. At that time the rationale for the conflict featured the so-called domino theory that assumed communism was flowing into Vietnam from China and would overtake Southeast Asia. Chinese troops were present in numbers in North Vietnam. Fifty years later, I had a conversation with one of the Chinese generals involved with the Sanya Initiative about the Vietnam War. It became clear that he and I had been in roughly the same part of Vietnam, and US and Chinese forces were engaged at the same time. I came to know this Chinese general quite well and met his wife and family. We agreed on the importance of never again winding up on opposite sides of a shooting war. I learned during my exchanges with senior PLA officers that older Chinese men like to hold hands. Following one discussion in the Sanya Initiative, as we headed to a dinner with our wives, the Chinese general reached over to take my hand. I am not reluctant to admit that I liked the personal gesture and pray that our children can hold hands as we look toward the future of US–China relations. We cannot afford to do otherwise.

Both China and the United States will change over the next two decades, and the rate of change is likely to accelerate, particularly considering what some refer to as the Fourth Industrial Revolution and the prospect of climate change. I've used the notion of a "surprise-free projection" for the next 20 years. This approach does not rest on a single perspective of the future, but rather a spread of events. It focuses largely on what would not be surprising for changes in China and between the US and China.

The first two chapters of this book focus largely on China. The third chapter discusses the military relationship between the US and China. The fourth chapter looks at the range of surprise-free relationships between the two nations, how to shape a beneficial future for each one, and how to avoid war.

NOTES

1. Neta Crawford, "United States Budgetary Costs of the Post-9/11 Wars Through FY2019" (Watson Institute for International and Public Affairs, Brown University, 2018); https://watson.brown.edu/costsofwar/files/cow/imce/papers/2018/Crawford_Costs%20of%20War%20Estimates%20Through%20FY2019.pdf.
2. Nongovernmental, informal, and unofficial contacts and activities between private citizens or groups of individuals.
3. Together with other American participants, I discuss the Sanya Initiative meetings with senior US military and civilian officials. No doubt, the Chinese participants also do the same with their governmental officials.

CHAPTER 1

A SOCIETY ON THE FAST TRACK: RISE OF THE DRAGON

Demography

The future of China depends on its people. Between 1959 and 1961, which were known as the "three years of famine," about 36 million Chinese died of starvation. In the early 1960s, the average lifespan for a Chinese person was 44 years; by 2019 it was 76.[1] But the one-child policy decreed by Deng Xiaoping in 1979 restricted population growth. The policy was not all-encompassing and largely affected ethnic Han Chinese in urban areas. It remained a temporary measure for 36 years, precluding the birth of 300 million people. A cultural preference for males combined with abortion, out-of-country adoption, and neglect of female infants contributed to a ratio of 115 males for every 100 females among newborns. This skewed ratio (instead of 105 males to 100 females) produced a generation of men who did not have enough women to marry and bear children. So-called "forever bachelors" are completing their working years without a family to care for them in old age. The total fertility rate among Chinese is 1.6 children per woman, whereas 2.1 is the replacement level of fertility, representing a stable population, exclusive of the migration from other nations. (See Fig. 1.)

Demographic Foundation

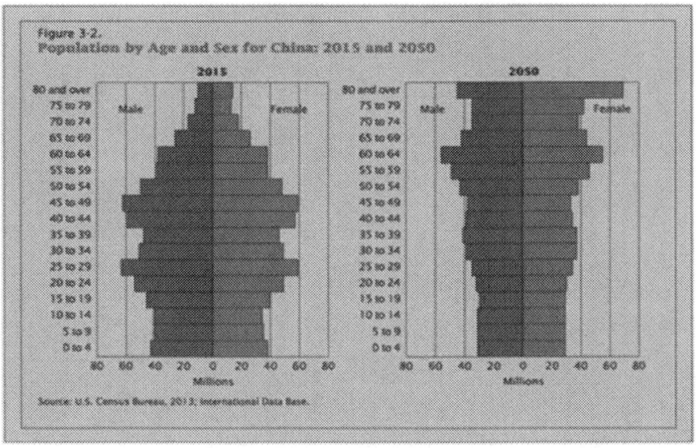

Figure 1

I met Chang during a graduate seminar at Beijing University. During a break, I asked why he was there, as he looked older than the other students. He said he was in his 40s and in school to get a better-paying job (after working as a journalist with *The People's Daily*). He said he wanted to get married and live in Beijing. The problem was that the single women in Beijing simply would not marry a man who could not afford housing in the city. He said that behind this was a huge cultural shift on the part of women who were no longer willing to move into their in-law's house, which was viewed as a traditional means of "helping" the mother-in-law. "The times, they are a-changing" he said, smiling.

Today in China, the working population has about five workers for each nonworker, which will decrease to about two workers for each nonworker over the next two decades.[2] (See Fig. 2.) In a macro sense, the per-capita workers must become more productive to provide the Social Security benefits for older generations who tend to live longer than their parents. These facts have serious implications for China's demographics. Many young couples no longer want to have more than one child while they are seeking to secure a better economic future. In order to support the elderly as the working population declines, it requires rigorous planning on Social Security support while raising the productivity level of the working population.

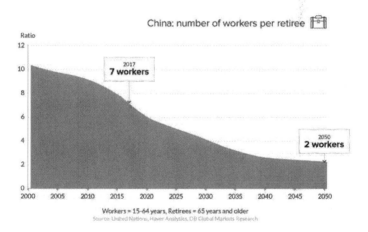

Figure 2

The Middle Class

Since the early 2000s, the middle class in China has become one of the most rapidly growing in the world, having increased from 29 million in 1999 (2% of the population) to about 531 million in 2013 (39% of the population). It is worth noting that the jump occurred largely in the lower-middle income band. (See Fig. 3 for further insight on this trend.)

The income disparity in China ranks as one of the highest in the world: The richest households (1%) own one-third of national wealth, and the poorest households (25%) own just 1%,[3] and there is little sign of abating. The urban rich seem to be getting richer while the rural poor are lagging behind.

China's Middle Class as Percent of Urban Households

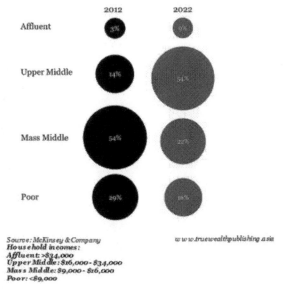

Figure 3

Education

Through implementation of the Law of Nine-Year Compulsory Education[4] enacted in 1986, China has overcome illiteracy among young and middle-aged citizens. However, has not ensured equality of education. Students from affluent backgrounds and urban areas generally have greater access to high-quality education than those from lower-income families and rural areas. Moreover, the policy on financing education requires local government to partially bear the burden of funding schools that often lack the funds to pay teachers, purchase instructional material, and maintain facilities, which makes it difficult to maintain schools in the rural regions. The migration from rural to urban areas decreased the number of primary schools in villages from 668,685 in 1995 to 201,377 in 2014. This urban–rural disparity also extends to student–teacher ratios in primary and secondary schools. While the average number of students per teacher[5] in Beijing and Shanghai is 15:1 and 14:1, respectively, which is roughly similar to New York and Los Angeles, Chinese classrooms outside the major cities generally have ratios of many more students per teacher.

The National Plan for Medium – and Long-term Education Reform and Development (2010–2020) emphasized scientific and technological innovation.[6] Yet educational access remains uneven. Data from the National Bureau of Statistics suggested that urban residents who have access to better schools enjoy a threefold income advantage over rural counterparts.[7] China has made considerable strides over the past decade in postsecondary school learning with the support of universities, technical training institutes, community colleges, and research laboratories. It has more than doubled the number of tertiary education institutions.

Cultivating highly skilled workers is crucial for the Chinese transition to an innovation-based economy. The National Medium – and Long-Term Talent Development Plan (2010–2020) vowed to improve coordination between tertiary education and labor markets. It aims to create higher-education research facilities in central and western provinces, increase spending on human resources from 10.75 to 15% percent of GDP, and raise the tertiary enrollment rate to 40% percent by 2020.[8] Effective implementation of the Talent Development Plan may prove critical as the Chinese seek to transition from manufacturing to global innovation. In terms of international students, there were more than 369,000 Chinese attending US colleges and universities during the 2018–2019 academic year. They were the largest number of foreign students.[9]

Urbanization

More than half of China's 1.4 billion population live in cities, and the administrations divide the urban areas in terms of population: "megacities" (such as Beijing, Shanghai, Guangzhou, and Shenzhen), "large cities," and other city categories based on populations. The 18th National Congress of the CPC has announced integrated urban–rural development, and China will deepen household registration reforms, relax restrictions on urban settlement except for several megacities, promote coordinated development between cities and towns, as well as increase the population-carrying capacity and attractiveness of mid – and small-sized cities. To achieve these goals, China will break barriers that restrict the free flow of resources— such as capital, talents, and information—between urban and rural areas, and inject new impetus to the countryside. It will seek to deepen and improve rural land reform and allow farmers to turn their land-use rights into shares in farming enterprises or cooperatives. To promote diversified economic development in rural areas, the country will continue to protect its agriculture, establish a cultivation mechanism for new industries, and build a platform for integrated development of urban and rural industries.[10]

The rush to acquire land for development is visible in so-called ghost cities, which are areas of urban expansion with the hallmarks of modern cities but without residents.[11] In a speech to the 19th Party Congress in 2017, General Secretary Xi Jinping said housing is intended to be lived in, not bought and sold for speculation. His remarks were meant to caution speculators and warn that the issue might be targeted by his anti-corruption campaign.

Economics

In 2013, the World Bank teamed with Chinese governmental research agencies to forecast the Chinese economy through 2030. There is some likelihood that Xi drew from the resulting study, *China 2030: Building a Modern, Harmonious, and Creative Society*, particularly its discussion of the middle-income trap.[12] (See Figs. 4A and B.)

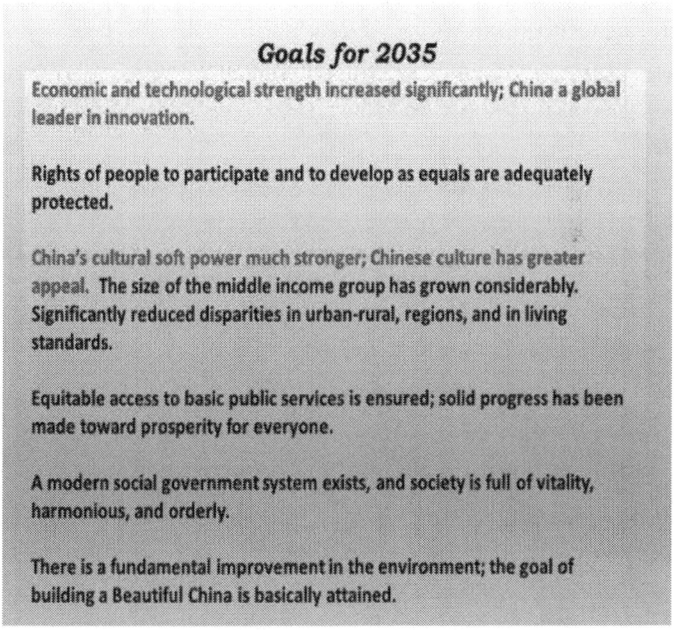

Goals for 2035

Economic and technological strength increased significantly; China a global leader in innovation.

Rights of people to participate and to develop as equals are adequately protected.

China's cultural soft power much stronger; Chinese culture has greater appeal. The size of the middle income group has grown considerably. Significantly reduced disparities in urban-rural, regions, and in living standards.

Equitable access to basic public services is ensured; solid progress has been made toward prosperity for everyone.

A modern social government system exists, and society is full of vitality, harmonious, and orderly.

There is a fundamental improvement in the environment; the goal of building a Beautiful China is basically attained.

Figure 4A: Goals for 2035, Xi Jinping Points from Speech at 19th Party Conference.

Leader in Innovation

China will....

* strengthen basic research in applied sciences, launch major national science and technology projects, and prioritize innovation in modern engineering technologies, and disruptive technologies. These efforts will provide powerful support for building China's strength in science and technology, product quality, aerospace, cyberspace, and transportation; and for building a digital China and a smart society.

* develop a market-oriented system for technological innovation in which enterprises are the main players and synergy is created through the joint efforts of enterprises, universities, and research institutes. We will support innovation by small and medium-sized enterprises and encourage the application of advances in science and technology.

* foster a culture of innovation, and strengthen the creation, protection, and application of intellectual property. We should cultivate a large number of world-class scientists and technologists in strategically important fields, scientific and technological leaders, and young scientists and engineers, as well as high-performing innovation teams.

Figure 4B: Goals for 2035, Xi Jinping Points from Speech at 19th Party Conference.

The study focused on the postwar era, arguing that a number of nations had moved rapidly into middle-income status, but far fewer had gone on to high-income status. Instead, they had been unable to get out of what the researchers named the middle-income trap. The nations had risen into the middle income based on low-cost labor and easy, well-understood technology. This was the trigger for other nations to follow the same route. As countries reached middle-income levels, the underemployed rural labor force dwindled and wages increased, eroding competitiveness. The nations that escaped the trap (Japan, South Korea, and a few others) did so by focusing on new technology.

One of the responses was the "Made in China 2025," announced by Li Keqiang, Premier of the State Council of the People's Republic in 2015 as an important means of avoiding the middle-income trap. It identified the goal of leadership in ten emerging technologies: robotics, ships, railway transport, next-generation vehicles, aircraft and space, medicine, new materials, electronics, energy equipment, and agriculture equipment. It also recommended getting results for China's domestic goals and leadership in the world in these technologies in order to avoid the middle-income trap.

China is laying the groundwork to acquire scarce resources overseas and to sell competitively in a multipolar international economy. It is continuing to develop industries capable of competing on their own without direct government support and subsidies. Thus far, this competitiveness has been limited to high-tech areas with Alibaba, Tencent, and Baidu successfully listed on international exchanges. Centralized control over the banking system also has contributed to infrastructure development in a more systemic way compared to the United States where the public sector is less involved in replacing infrastructure. As a result, the Chinese investment in infrastructure may outpace projects within the United States.

However, this historic transformation still is not on a clear trajectory nine years after the global financial crisis, reflecting a period that was dominated by rural-to-urban migration and industrialization that drove a building boom, raised living standards, and produced capital surpluses that helped to fund borrowing worldwide. The Chinese population is aging rapidly, and its growth will be complicated by domestic overcapacity, high debt, and vulnerable banking practices. The rest of the world, particularly developing nations, must adjust to a China that is no longer a center of ever-growing commodity demand, but is instead a more balanced trading partner.

I place my strong bet on China's ability to persevere despite these many challenges, and to take its place as the largest economy in the world. We must acknowledge all China has accomplished economically to be where it is, as well as the challenges it has faced to get there, and know that the country is poised to move ahead as it has planned.

Xi rose to power in late 2012. So far, he has expressed little interest in Western-style political or economic reform. In early 2013 Document No. 9[13] was distributed within the Communist Party outlining threats including constitutional democracy, universal human rights, pro-market neoliberalism, and Western ideas of media independence and civic participation. It concluded that ideological debates between infiltration and anti-infiltration remained severe, but if Communist Party leadership and socialism persisted, Western anti-China efforts would continue. As a result of such threats, China could not let down its guard or decrease its vigilance.

Party Factions
Ninety million people within one party do not all think or act the same. The Communist Party is extremely hierarchal; the politburo dictates policy, and subparty levels carry it out and report to higher levels on progress or lack of progress in implementing the policies. According to party rules, all party members must be nominated by members, and other members decide whether a candidate can begin a one-year period of probation, after which they become a full party member. (General Secretary Xi reportedly failed several times in this process.) Members identified as outstanding receive support from senior members and normally go on to attend the party university in Beijing.

Confucianism influences Chinese politics through the creation of social ties (*guanxi*). Five categories of social ties can create political factions: family, birthplace, college, work experience, and becoming the personal secretary to a senior official form the roots of Communist Party factions. The rule of avoidance used to circumvent *guanxi* has become the norm in party matters. This requires that party cadres not be assigned to important posts in their birthplaces where they could easily build factions among family members, old friends, and longtime colleagues. However, the rule of avoidance is not equally enforced in every province. It is effectively implemented in deep-in-debt provinces that rely on government financial relief. But in affluent provinces, the native officials are much better positioned to get key posts on provincial standing committees.

After the leadership transition in 2012, Xi Jinping, the new general secretary of the Communist Party, initiated a far-reaching anti-corruption campaign with the slogan "swatting flies and killing tigers." The tigers are high-ranking officials who are rumored to consist of about 350 senior members. Estimates of the anti-corruption campaign report dealing with about one million junior party members. Xi appears concerned about this widespread corruption that is dangerous to the legitimacy of the Communist Party, and the anti-corruption campaign could bring him personal benefits by increasing public support. It also sets the course for more viable leadership in the country as it becomes one of the two largest economies and leaders in the world along with the United States. The arrest of Zhou Yongkang, a former member of the Standing Committee and head of internal security, for both corruption and abuse of power demonstrated the anti-corruption campaign's wide scope. The event broke a post-Mao norm whereby retired politburo members should be exempt from legal investigation and prosecution. However, factional arrangements are important within the Communist Party, and the stakes are high.

Xi has moved swiftly since coming to power in 2012, generating an extensive anti-corruption campaign in both the Communist Party and the People's Liberation Army (PLA). The two highest-ranking general officers—former Vice Chairmen of the Central Military Commission (CMC)—were jailed for corruption in 2014 and 2015. In addition, some 900,000 officials and 1,600 officers were disciplined by 2017. As the general secretary of the Communist Party, Xi advocated for PLA reorganization and budget adjustments mainly at the expense of ground forces. In addition, he sponsored new concepts and strategies in his role as the CMC chairman.

Future Visions

It is most important that our policymakers grasp a deeper understanding of the People's Republic of China's future and how that future will affect the United States. There seems to be a recognition that there have been three stages of China's development associated with an individual: Mao Zedong, Deng Xiaoping, and now Xi Jinping, each with power, vision, and longevity.

Elizabeth C. Economy's *The Third Revolution: Xi Jinping and the New Chinese State* focused "on how different is a Xi-led China from those that preceded him?" Her study argued that it was certainly different enough to warrant a new revolution in China that would shake the world. Early on in his position as general secretary, Xi called for the revival and rejuvenation of the Chinese nation and its "indelible contribution" to world civilization.[14]

NOTES

1. Macrotrends; "China Life Expectancy 1950-2020;" https://www.macrotrends.net/countries/CHN/china/life-expectancy.
2. United Nations, Haver Analytics, DB Global Markets.
3. The World Bank; "GINI index (World Bank estimate) – China;" https://data.worldbank.org/indicator/SI.POV.GINI?end=2015&locations=CN&name_desc=true&start=1990&view=chart.
4. China.org.cn; "Historic Achievements: 60 Years of Educational Reform and Development;" www.china.org.cn/government/scio-press-conferences/2009-09/11/content_18508942.htm.
5. China Statistics Press; "China Statistical Yearbook 2015;" www.stats.gov.cn/tjsj/ndsj/2015/indexeh.htm.
6. United Nations Educational, Scientific and Cultural Organization; "Outline of China's national plan for medium and long-term education reform and development 2010-2020;" https://planipolis.iiep.unesco.org/en/2010/outline-chinas-national-plan-medium-and-long-term-education-reform-and-development-2010-2020.
7. *The Economist*; Up on the farm: Rising rural incomes are making China more equal;" https://www.economist.com/finance-and-economics/2016/05/13/up-on-the-farm.
8. The Brookings Institution; "China's National Talent Plan: Key Measures and Objectives;" https://www.brookings.edu/research/chinas-national-talent-plan-key-measures-and-objectives/.
9. Statista; "Number of college and university students from China in the United States from academic year 2008/09 to 2018/19;" https://www.statista.com/statistics/372900/number-of-chinese-students-that-study-in-the-us/.
10. Xinhuanet; "China announces guidelines to promote integrated urban-rural development;" http://www.xinhuanet.com/english/2019-05/06/c_138036240.htm.
11. Intercollegiate Finance Journal; "What Has Become of China's Ghost Cities;" http://www.the-ifj.com/2019/02/06/what-has-become-of-chinas-ghost-cities/a.

12. World Bank and the Development Research Center of the State Council; "China 2030: Building a Modern, Harmonious, and Creative Society;" http://documents.worldbank.org/curated/en/781101468239669951/China-2030-building-a-modern-harmonious-and-creative-society.

13. *The New York Times*; "China Takes Aim at Western Ideas;" https://www.nytimes.com/2013/08/20/world/asia/chinas-new-leadership-takes-hard-line-in-secret-memo.html?pagewanted=all&_r=1&.

14. Elizabeth C. Economy, *The Third Revolution: Xi Jinping and China State* (Oxford: Oxford University Press, 2018).

CHAPTER 2

CHINA JOINS THE WORLD ORDER: TO CHANGE IT

The People's Republic of China was denied participation in most international organizations in the first two decades of its existence largely because of US opposition in the wake of the Chinese Civil War. In 1971, however, Beijing took the Chinese seat at the United Nations as relations with the US improved. After entering the UN, China joined most of its affiliated bodies, including the World Bank and the International Monetary Fund. The willingness of China to open to the outside world accelerated during the late 1970s. The country received economic and technical assistance from the United Nations Development Programme, marking a departure from its previous commitment to self-reliance. In 1986, China applied for a seat on the General Agreement on Tariffs and Trade (GATT) as a founding member.

By the late 1980s, China held memberships in hundreds of international and regional organizations, including the International Atomic Energy Agency (IAEA), World Intellectual Property Organization (WIPO), and International Olympic Committee (IOC) plus associations or societies that focused on narrow issues such as acrobatics and seaweed. Besides providing a forum to express its views, membership in a growing number of international groups in the 1970s and 1980s afforded Chinese diplomats and other officials international knowledge and experience. China did not seek membership in some important international organizations representing interests of the third world: It skipped the Group of 77 and the Non-Aligned Movement. Despite the Chinese emphasis on its relations with the third world, the independent foreign policy and special position of Beijing resulted in its nonparticipation beyond observer status in these groups.

By the second half of the 1980s, China's participation in international organizations reflected two primary objectives of its independent foreign policy: furthering domestic economic development through cooperation with the outside world and promoting peace and stability by cultivating ties with other nations on an equal footing. Zhao Ziyang expressed views on this in a report presented to the National People's Congress: "China is a developing socialist country with a population of over one billion. We are well aware of our obligations and responsibilities ... [and] continue to work hard on both fronts, domestic and international, to push forward the socialist modernization of our country and to make greater contributions to world peace and human progress."[1]

In recent decades, China's support for the United Nations has grown considerably. China is now the third largest contributor to the United Nations' regular budget,[2] the second largest contributor to the peacekeeping budget,[3] and has committed more than 2,500 personnel[4] to UN peacekeeping operations as of 2018. Multilateral organizations like the UN foster cooperation between countries and can facilitate diplomatic and political solutions to a range of transnational and subnational problems. The UN, therefore, provides China with a collaborative forum through which it can exert global influence. It also provides valuable training to its military through peacekeeping participation while promoting a positive image of China. Given the United Nations' mandate for upholding international peace, China's participation in UN operations offers Beijing a low-cost means of demonstrating its commitment to global stability, thereby allaying concerns over China's growing military and economic strength.[5] Between 1971 (when China became a permanent member of the United Nations Security Council) and 2019, China used 12 vetoes, the least of any permanent member.

Peacekeeping Activities

China abstained from voting at the United Nations on peacekeeping resolutions and from contributing funds for peacekeeping operations until 1981 and only sent its first peacekeepers to Cambodia in 1992. A landmark in Chinese participation as a provider of global security came in 2015. Not only did General Secretary Xi commit 8,000 personnel to the UN peacekeeping standby force that represented one-fifth of the 40,000 total troops committed by fifty nations, but China also pledged $100 million to the African Standby Force (ASF) and $1 billion to the United Nations Peace and Development Trust Fund. The decision by China to commit troops to UN peacekeeping missions is most likely part of China's emphasis on global involvement. It roughly coincided with the Olympic Games of 2008 held in Beijing, the start of the Belt and Road Initiative (BRI), the expansion of territorial claims in the South China Sea, and the initial militarization of manmade islands. Unlike other nations that contribute to multiple peacekeeping operations with ad hoc groups, regional organizations, or alliances, China only engages in missions through the United Nations. Also, it is the only UN Security Council member to exercise its veto while identifying as a great power and a developing country. The Chinese tend to deploy "enabler troops" such as medical, engineering, and logistic personnel who provide the support to peacekeeping missions. These assets are typically sparse in the militaries of developing countries and expensive to maintain and train.

Belt and Road Initiative

Since announced by Xi in 2013, the BRI has been China's broadest effort to participate in the world order, an order largely designed and initiated by the United States in the past century. China has explained the effort as a modern Chinese "Marshall Plan." Others have argued it is a Chinese state-backed policy for global dominance, or an offset package for a slowing economy and a massive marketing campaign for something that was already happening—Chinese investment around the world. The legitimacy of this project was questioned. Does it represent a grand vision for intercontinental access or a veiled attempt to offload excess capacity? Is it intended to develop global military capabilities? A means to monopolize cyber-sovereignty and artificial intelligence? The answer is "yes" to all of the above. (See Fig. 5.)

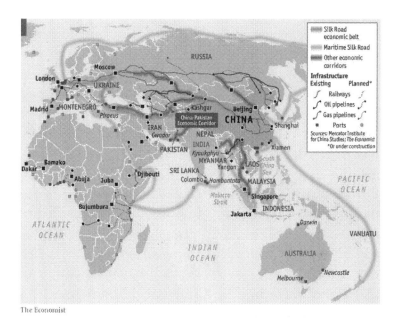

The Economist

Figure 5: Belt and Road Initiative.

It became the signature foreign policy and geo-economic initiative of Xi Jinping, who dubbed it the project of the century. Since its inception in 2013, the BRI has a major policy agenda in Beijing as a well-resourced, whole-of-government concept for regional and global interconnectivity. Just what that means has yet to come into focus, although its intent is clear: encourage development and influence outlying provinces, expand markets and export technical standards, build hard infrastructure, bolster energy security, expand military presence in order to protect interests abroad, and advance geopolitical influence. Furthermore, it has security implications for the United States and its allies and partners, including the expansion of Chinese military power, overseas presence, and access to foreign ports. It also challenges US and allied interests and international rules-based order predicated on open markets and democratic governance. Many nations raised concern over exacerbating debt and undermining transparency. The United States and like-minded nations are working to develop responses that strike a balance between engagement in BRI as a way of meeting global infrastructure requirements while countering economic and strategic risks.

Inaugurated in 2013 to encourage policy coordination, facilitate connectivity, expand trade, integrate financial transactions, and foster people-to-people exchanges, the BRI has become the keystone of Chinese foreign policy and a major component of Chinese economic planning. In October 2017, the Chinese leadership demonstrated the importance they place on this project when they wrote it into the constitution. Broadly speaking, the land-based belt runs from China through Central and South Asia and the Middle East to Europe. The sea-based road connects China with South Asia, the Middle East, East Africa, and Europe via sea lanes passing through the South China Sea, Indian Ocean, Red Sea, Suez Canal, and Eastern Mediterranean. However, it is not limited to two routes. The Chinese vision includes Latin America and the Caribbean, the Arctic, and even space—although plans for activities in those regions are less developed. By investing in infrastructure, Xi hopes to find a more profitable home for the vast Chinese foreign reserves, most of which is invested in US government securities. He hopes to create new markets for high-speed rail firms and export the vast amounts of excess capacity in cement, steel, and other metals. By investing in volatile countries in Central Asia, he is building a more stable neighborhood for restive provinces such as Xinjiang and

Tibet. Moreover, by encouraging more Chinese projects around the South China Sea, the BRI could bolster claims within that region.

These various motivations can create conflicting interests. Infighting exists among important Chinese institutions including the Ministry of Commerce, the Foreign Ministry, the Planning Commission, and various provincial governments. Overall, China is experiencing a backlash against some of its plans, with Malaysia, Myanmar, and Sri Lanka either repudiating or attempting to renegotiate Chinese projects approved by their former administrations.

Beijing's rationale is that by boosting connectivity, China can spur growth in the short term, gain access to valuable natural resources in the midterm, and create new booming markets for its goods in the far future. One goal is to use infrastructure as a means of projecting and building regional influence. Building infrastructure at scale is something that China has demonstrated it can do, and its state-owned enterprises (SOEs) that modernized infrastructure megaprojects in China are actively engaged in similar efforts associated with the BRI. It is also an important part of Chinese trade and investment initiatives that seek to advance regional economic integration and promote greater economic reliance on China.

Estimates made by the Asian Development Bank (ADB) for developing nations collectively amounted to some $26 trillion in various infrastructure investments between 2016 and 2030. Over the past five years, the BRI has expanded in scope and number to encompass more than 80 participating nations that represented roughly 30% of the gross domestic product of the world. It is linked to goals set by Beijing to align the global political and economic order with its geopolitical interests. Some goals such as fueling domestic development, expanding markets and exporting technical standards, and building hard and digital infrastructure have been explicitly stated in official policy communiques. Other goals such as furthering strategic ambitions by bolstering energy security, protecting overseas interests, and advancing geopolitical influence are less deliberated except by Australia, Japan, South Korea, and the United States.

China Standards 2035

The 19th National Congress report stated that by 2035, China seeks to "become a global leader in innovation." (See Fig. 4B.) This ambition is important for three reasons. First, leadership in technological innovation increases the likelihood that a country will enjoy higher productivity and wealth than its peers. Second, the transferability between military and civilian technology means that a technologically advanced country is better positioned to build a premier military—an idea captured in the report's directives for "military-civilian fusion." Third, technological leadership enhances a country's international influence, or "soft power," because others tend to emulate the world's technological leader and the lifestyle changes it affords.[6]

To dominate cutting-edge technologies like artificial intelligence (AI), cloud computing, IoT (Internet of Things), and big data, China intends to accelerate efforts to develop technical standards, with an eye toward exporting them to the international market, and thus "China Standards 2035" has arrived.[7]

Four main subjects are discussed in the "China Standards 2035" project: the importance of standards (the position and goal of standardization strategy), the Chinese standardization system, method and evaluation, the strategy of a standardization system supporting high-quality development, and the standardization strategy of civil-military harmonized development. By January 2020 the conclusion materials will be generated, and they are expected to provide suggestions to the CPC Central Committee and the State Council about moving forward with implementing the standardization strategy.

Soft Power

Soft power is usually defined as the ability of one nation to affect the actions of another nation through appeal and attraction, rather than coercion (hard power). The currency of soft power is culture, political values, and, assistance. Recently, the term has also been used in changing and influencing social and public opinion through relatively less transparent channels and through powerful political and nonpolitical organizations.

China's interest in soft power started to develop as early as 1993, at a time when China needed to counteract the "China Threat" theory, which had gained traction overseas after China introduced its 1992 Territorial Sea Law, formally claiming much of the East and South China seas and many of their islands. China was initially concerned about the infiltration of "American values," but over the next two decades it began to develop a more comprehensive conception of Chinese values, based on a mixture of modern Marxist values—so-called "socialist core values"— and traditional Confucian values. In his report for the 17th

National Congress in 2007, former President Hu Jintao outlined the importance of both the socialist value system and of the promotion of Chinese culture, including the need to encourage cultural connectivity among the Chinese people. The report explicitly referred to soft power, marking the first time this term had been used in an official document since the establishment of the People's Republic of China.[8] Seven years later, in 2014, General Secretary Xi Jinping formally endorsed the concept, calling for a stronger national effort to boost China's global popularity in proportion to its economic rise: "We should increase China's soft power, give a good Chinese narrative and better communicate China's message to the world." Three years later, in 2017, Xi outlined in Davos the root causes for the widening gaps in the global economy and implied China's willingness to step into the leadership position to expand global trade that the US had vacated.

China's efforts to boost its soft power abroad cost about $10 billion US dollars annually, including funding programs such as the Confucius Institutes, which began in 2004 seeking to promote Chinese language and culture, support local Chinese teaching internationally, and facilitate cultural exchanges. To influence public opinion, China has also supported its state-run foreign language news media in circulating a well-managed narrative about the country, with their ever-expanding global reach. The Xinhua News Agency has more than 160 bureaus worldwide, while CCTV International—rebranded as the China Global Television Network—broadcasts in English, Spanish, French, Arabic, and Russian. Chinese media have also supported training courses for journalists from Asia, Africa, and Latin America.

In recent years, China has been attempting to export its approach to development via BRI, as a vehicle for promoting soft power while boosting economic integration between Asia, the Middle East, Africa, and Europe. Through BRI, China has been pursuing more cooperation with other countries via the Regional Comprehensive Economic Partnership (RCEP), which has 16 signatory nations as of 2019. This agreement will account for almost 50% of the world's population and more than 30% of global GDP. This demonstrates China's leadership role in defending multilateral trade mechanisms in the face of US protectionist tendencies, and in doing so, further expands its international soft power campaign.

NOTES

1. Robert L. Worden, Andrea Matles Savada, and Ronald E. Dolan, eds., *China: A Country Study* (Washington: GPO for the Library of Congress, 1987), "China's Role in International Organizations;" http://countrystudies.us/china/.

2. United Nations; "Assessment of Member States' contributions to the United Nations regular budget for the year 2017;" https://www.un.org/ga/search/view_doc.asp?symbol=ST/ADM/SER.B/955.

3. United Nations; "Scale of assessments for the apportionment of the expenses of United Nations peacekeeping operations;" https://www.un.org/en/ga/search/view_doc.asp?symbol=A/70/331/Add.1.

4. ChinaPower; "UN Peacekeeping Mission Contributions;" https://chinapower.csis.org/data/un-peacekeeping-mission-contributions.

5. ChinaPower; "Is China contributing to the United Nations' Mission?;" https://chinapower.csis.org./china-un-mission.

6. Timothy R. Heath, "China's Endgame: The Path Towards Global Leadership," *The Lawfare Institute* (blog), January 5, 2018, https://www.lawfareblog.com/chinas-endgame-path-towards-global-leadership.

7.   The SECEC Project; "24/05/2018 Chinese Standards 2035, the standardization strategy research is kicked off;" https://www.sesec.eu/24-05-2018-chinese-standards-2035-the-standardization-strategy-research-is-kicked-off/.

8.   Osamu Sayama, "China's Approach to Soft Power: Seeking a Balance between Nationalism, Legitimacy and International Influence," Royal United Services Institute for Defence and Security Studies, March 17, 2016, https://www.cf https://rusi.org/sites/default/files/201603_op_chinas   r.org/backgrounder/chinas-big-bet-soft-power.

CHAPTER 3

THE 20-YEAR MILITARY BALANCE: CHINA AND US MILITARIES ENTER THE FOURTH INDUSTRIAL REVOLUTION

Regretfully, the US and Chinese militaries are already contemplating how to fight each other. Institutionally, China has shifted emphasis to the future sooner than the United States, largely because we have been engaged in conflicts for the past 17 years. Both are focused on modernization with emphasis on offsetting capabilities. America expresses interest in anti-access/area denial (A2/AD), but the PLA counter-term for this strategic concept is multidomain operations. This chapter focuses on what we will see as the interactions of our two military forces.

Much of the technology needed by the US military to conduct A2/AD and for the PLA's multidomain operations does not yet exist: 1,000-mile hypersonic missiles, high-speed helicopters, robotic logistics, and above all smart networks that are required to coordinate. (For example, Sydney J. Freedberg Jr., deputy editor for *Breaking Defense*, described an Air Force hacker tricking enemy radar to ignore a Navy fighter pilot as he strikes a target spotted by an Army Ranger with artificially intelligent eyewear.) What these concepts emphasize is covering a grey zone arena prior to direct combat. This concept, enshrined in the *National Defense Strategy* of former Secretary of Defense James Mattis as "competition," is distinct from conflict. It is the arena in which hacking, espionage, covert operations, and electronic probes cooperate to stimulate enemy sensors, tricking them into turning on so you can study how they work and where they are. It also includes the notion of calibrated force posture of increasing depth and timeliness regarding the capabilities of an opponent, derived by integrating cyber operations, satellites, and other means of information, woven together by artificial intelligence and quantum computing. Its goals are to know what an opponent's forces are doing, planning, preparing for, and trying to assure the opponent can't do the same thing to us. (Remarks by Secretary of Defense, James Mattis on the "National Defense Strategy in January 2018).[1]

China began major military modernization in the last decade of the twentieth century, driven in part by US capabilities demonstrated in Operations Desert Shield/Desert Storm. During the 1990s, the Pentagon wrestled with what was called a revolution in military affairs that essentially considered implications of information technology including computers, sensors, precision-guided weapons, and advanced communications. Chinese military personnel—both active and retired—wrote about this development and argued in favor of PLA attention to what was underway in the United States. By 2004, the Chinese military was embracing information technology as informatized capabilities, focused on getting information to those who need it to coordinate operations. At least that seemed to be true when the white paper *China's*

National Defense in 2004 was released.[2] The focus of the shift was exploitation of information technology and computer applications, particularly among the various PLA components that were moving toward conducting joint operations.

Fight and Win

Consider the statement by the Research Department of Military Strategy of the People's Liberation Army in 2013 after Xi became the Communist Party general secretary and Chairman of the Central Military Commission: "the most likely military conflict would be a large-scale, sudden attack by a strong adversary [presumably the United States] aimed at the PLA Navy and Air Force. It would not use nuclear weaponry but would use forces in the air, space, cyberspace, and maritime domains. The attacker would probably have planned for a preemptive attack in the belief that it possesses superior military capabilities vis-à-vis the opposition forces." (See Fig. 6.)

China's General Military Strategy

"...possibility of a large-scale ground invasion by an adversary is minimum.

"... target of high-technological warfare, such as air-naval, air-space, and space-cyber wars, is intensifying.

"...The threat from the east is more severe than that from the west, the threat from the sea is more severe than that from the ground; the threat from space and cyber network is gradually becoming true.

"...most severe war threat is a large-scale strategic sudden attack launched by a strong adversary, which aims at destroying our war potential.

"...The war we need to prepare for, particularly given the background of nuclear deterrence, is a large-scale, and highly intensive local war from the sea."

Figure 6

In late 2015, China announced major changes in the PLA force structure, organization, training, and operational roles (see Figs. 7 and 8). It was the most extensive reorganization since 1950 and was driven by three objectives: expanding and deepening oversight by the CMC; centralizing military training and placing training under control of regional commands; and creating five services: PLA (ground forces), Navy, Air Force, Rocket Force, and the Strategic Support Force. In the process, many activities were moved under the CMC bureaucracy, but this did not prevent the PLA from performing functions controlled by the CMC. The changes were reminiscent of what the United States did over the past 70 years, such as establishing the US Air Force as a separate service in 1949; the efforts by Secretary of Defense McNamara in the 1960s to shift decision responsibility on force structure, systems analyses, and five-year defense planning; and the Goldwater–Nichols Act of 1986, which fostered jointness in the US Armed Forces. China is attempting similar things.

Figure 1. PLA Structure Prior to Reform

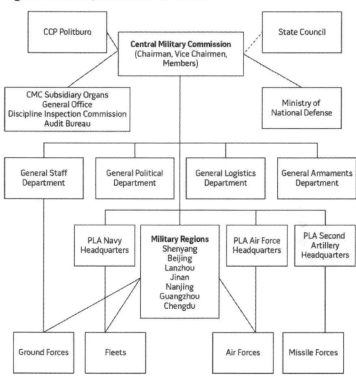

Figure 7

Figure 2. PLA Structure after Reform

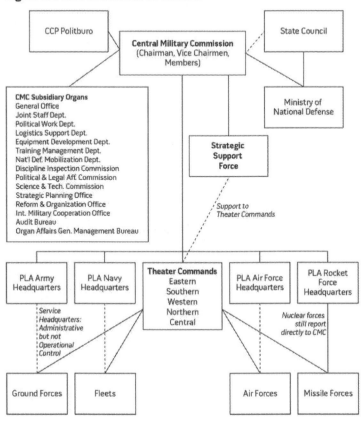

Figure 8

The most relevant transition by the People's Liberation Army has been the shift from a land warfare orientation to a maritime-centric force capable of fighting and winning in the near seas (South and East China Seas) by 2035 and a force that can fight and win globally by the middle of the twenty-first century. Some analysts believe that the Belt and Road Initiative, particularly regarding port facilities, is associated with potential military basing outside China.

The United States and China will continue to develop, test, and modernize their militaries. Aircraft in 2039 will fly higher, faster, and be deadlier; ships will be more advanced; and land forces will be faster, better-armed, and better protected. But what is called the Fourth Industrial Revolution will provide disruptive technologies, driven by robotics, AI, and quantum computing. (See Fig. 9.)

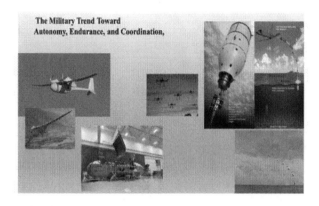

Figure 9

Addressing the 19th Communist Party Congress, Xi highlighted those capabilities: "We will adapt to the trend of a new global military revolution and to national security needs; we will upgrade our military capabilities, and see that, by the year 2020, mechanization is basically achieved, [information technology] application has come a long way, and strategic capabilities have seen a big improvement. In step with our country's modernization process, we will modernize our military across the board in terms of theory, organizational structure, service personnel, and weaponry. We will make it our mission to see that by 2035, the modernization of our national defense and our forces is basically completed; and that by the mid-twenty-first century our people's armed forces have been fully transformed into world-class forces."

Over the past decade, the Chinese military has developed informatized conditions of modern warfare to leverage communication connectivity, networks, and information and communication defenses. And, in the next two decades, the Chinese military will extend those advances with both cognitive autonomous capabilities and manufacturing techniques. The underlying technologies of the future have moved from the notion of informatized to the "intelligentization" (a term that increasingly appears to imply more accurate understanding of warfare based on computers, robotics, AI, and quantum sciences). The transformations are still being explored, developed, and tested, but China is investing in those technologies and their potential for a future conflict with the United States.

The Fourth Industrial Revolution will transform conflict by profoundly lifting the fog of war by means of artificial intelligence, robotics, quantum computing, and quantum communication. The success of Chinese technology companies such as Baidu, Alibaba, and Tencent, together with startups, demonstrated the dynamism of the private sector in AI. From speech and face recognition to self-driving cars, research is expanding. Every year tens of billions of dollars are spent in that endeavor. Though the military dimension of Chinese progress in artificial intelligence has remained opaque, significant efforts are being made in the use of fourth-generation technology by PLA research institutes and defense industries. The military realizes the disruptive potential from applications of AI, from unmanned weapons systems to command and control, and it anticipates that artificial intelligence eventually will alter the fundamental character of war. Recognizing its strategic implications, the Chinese prioritized AI. Progress was established through long-term research funded under national science and technology efforts such as the 863 Program. The 13th Five-Year Plan (2016–2020) called for breakthroughs in artificial intelligence that as highlighted in the 13th Five-Year National Science and Technology Innovation Plan. The Chinese Academy of Engineering proposed the Artificial Intelligence 2.0 Plan while the Ministry of Science and Technology will be developing AI through 2030. The obvious intensity of these efforts is likely to enable continued, rapidly for military applications. Xi also announced a surge of related programs at universities throughout China and abroad on the undergraduate and graduate levels to make the concepts operational. It is reminiscent of the National Defense Education Act passed in the Eisenhower Administration. However, the number of Chinese students is estimated at 100 times the number of those American students who similarly benefitted in the late 1950s and early 1960s.

Military Implications

Artificial intelligence can prompt the evolution of small, smart, and cheap weapons, able to communicate, identify, and track locations for a command or other drones. Moreover, it could attack opposing forces. Linked to robotics, the autonomy permits drones to be used in swarms. Both the United States and China are developing unmanned vehicles for operations on land, at (and beneath) sea, and in the air. Some will not require any external input other than signatures of designated targets with their routes and speed. They can be launched as precision strike weapons or positioned in an area to begin active hunting for prioritized targets. Both nations are doing substantial research and development on the fully autonomous warrior.

Military drones currently being developed will have ranges of up to three thousand miles with payloads of hundreds of pounds. Manufactured by three-dimensional printing with nano-explosives and AI, units could be fielded with capability of launching hundreds to thousands of smart drones in wave attacks beyond the range of ground fire support systems or tactical aircraft. For airpower, the problem will be protecting planes on the ground. An opponent does not have to deploy modern fighters or bombers. China is developing the conventional weapons capability to destroy US bases, ships, aircraft, and runways in Japan with combined ballistic and cruise missile attacks.

Within the next two decades a wide range of PLA units probably will be able to send hundreds of small drones to hunt American planes on expeditionary bases as well on their home base. Even if the aircraft themselves are protected by shelters, the radars, fuel systems, and ammunition dumps will remain highly vulnerable targets. Modern drones and cruise missiles can outrange fighter-bombers and strike airfields. They can push most air bases out of range of their targets. Though the United States operates a capable fleet of tankers, refueling orbits will remain in range of drones such as the XQ-222. Only bombers can outrange drones, but drones can be launched from commercial vessels and submarines to make bomber bases vulnerable.

The Maritime Domain

The US Navy has developed semiautonomous underwater gliders that can patrol for weeks. They surface periodically to report and receive new instructions. Similar drones are being purchased globally for about $100,000 each, and manufacturers are attempting to reduce their cost by 90%. The PLA Navy is developing and testing similar underwater gliders that can self-deploy torpedoes or mines. Defensively, they can establish smart minefields in maritime choke points. Also, they can be launched from various surface and subsurface platforms or remain secure ashore until needed, and then launch from a port or a beach. And they can plant sensors as well as act as one itself.

Warfare Circa 2039

The debate over the significance of the Fourth Industrial Revolution and its application to military affairs and strategy is underway in the United States and China. Artificial intelligence is going through its infancy in the military, but it will grow rapidly. Its potential stirs interest in both nations while some analysts caution that "intelligentization warfare" may stimulate a trend toward a "battlefield singularity" in which human intelligence may prove unable to keep abreast of the operational tempo of machine/computer warfare. As conflicts occur at machine/computer speed, inserting people in the loop that employs weapons or relies on human decision-making could become a liability rather than an asset. The issue of singularity as machines and computers take greater control in warfare gives pause to the militaries of both nations.

In a speech given to the 19th Communist Party Congress in 2017, Xi outlined the three-stage modernization of the

People's Liberation Army. The first will be completed in 2020, the second in the late 2030s, and the third in the 2050s. This assumes that the greatest danger that faces the Chinese military will occur in the next two decades and end in the late 2030s. PLA planners expect that the United States may launch a preemptive strike in the near seas by 2035. Xi and his advisors determined the goal of the second stage would be marked by deploying PLA units that can fight and win. But it is obvious that winning is linked to the near seas, at least for two decades. Based on that vision, the Chinese will build world-class military assets by mid-century. That does not mean war will no longer exist, but that relations between the PLA units and other world-class militaries would make a potential opponent less inclined to go to war with China.

The Chinese participants in the Sanya Initiative argue that America has sought to become a hegemon, increasingly dedicated to keeping China down by focusing on PLA strengths and weaknesses, and secretly planning surprise attacks. As such, they consider US efforts to access the near seas as an effort to gather military intelligence. They also believe that an arms race has begun and will accelerate. And their success will draw on the Fourth Industrial Revolution. In short, they believe in the vision outlined by Xi.

Warfare from Afar

Long-range, precision-guided missiles (both nuclear and nonnuclear) are proven technologies. Improvements in hypersonic vehicles and superguns remain in the experimental stage. But even the most precise and powerful weapons are impotent when you do not know where to shoot. The key component of a long-range missile system is not the missile, but sensors that find the targets and, above all, networks that transmit targeting data. The most effective way of stopping a missile is blinding sensors and disrupting networks. The Clausewitzian center of gravity in modern warfare is the network. It enables forces to disperse and seek cover to avoid precision fire and to coordinate their actions. It sends targeting data from scattered sensors to equally scattered weapons, combining efforts across vast distances to be focused on the decisive aim point. The disparities in a military confrontation between the United States and China in the South China Sea depend on sensors in space, seas, land and networks to coordinate offensive and defensive systems. Currently, the United States maintains an edge and likely will continue to maintain it for at least a decade.

The PLA observes the US military closely, not only in the near seas but also globally. It is deeply cognizant of developments across the US Armed Forces. It acknowledges the importance and superiority of American sensors and networks while believing it would be attacked on the mainland to counter land-based aircraft, command and control targets, and land-based antiaircraft systems. It perceives the greatest challenge is posed by the US Navy with its carriers. This has created PLA interest in hypersonic missiles, particularly maneuverable weapons. Given the mobility of a carrier task force and speed at which hypersonic missiles travel, the chances of hitting these moving targets are greater. But speed is only one of the many factors that increases the likelihood of hitting a moving target that is coupled with jamming efforts and artificial targets.

One consideration is a tactical nuclear weapon as a missile warhead, able to heavily damage surface ships within about a mile of detonation. That kind of notion stirs concern with nuclear escalation. But not as much as the first use of nuclear weapon on land with the prospect of higher civilian deaths.

The United States and China continue to develop capacities for stand-off and remote attacks. Both are developing cyberattack as well as precision-guided, robotic, and unmanned weapons that lower the threshold for initiating conflict because fewer lives are put at risk in efforts to overwhelm defenses. The proliferation of such weapons may shift conflicts away from direct clashes by opposing forces, especially during the initial phases. Future crises involving these weapons risk quick escalation because protagonists would be inclined to strike before they were attacked. Command, control, and targeting infrastructure, including satellites that can provide both navigation and targeting information, would be targeted by attacks seeking to disrupt opposition strike forces. Russia and China, for example, are pursuing weapons to destroy satellites, which places America at greater risk.

The US and Chinese militaries recognize this development and are directing research efforts to enhance cyber and space operations. Both are seeking means to attack networks and negate the information on targets generated by new and better sensors based in space and at sea. But activity in the space and cyber domains is changing. Space activity is increasingly driven by commercial projects to put satellites into earth orbit and more nations are taking advantage of the efforts. The number of satellites that provide communications and imaging is increasing, which will continue over the next decade. As a result, the amount of data of military use will increase dramatically on a global basis, particularly as AI provides insight and redundancy.

As space becomes more congested, it will be more contested. The immense strategic and commercial value of outer space assets ensures that many nations will compete for access, use, and control of space. The development and likely deployment of anti-satellite technologies are predictable despite emerging offsets. Space-based observation will get better in terms of adapting the electromagnet spectrum in new and better sensors. Placing them in orbit is becoming cheaper as commercial alternatives expand. And new satellites can be built that evade attack. But the most important breakthrough will be the use of AI processing of data from space-based sensors, airborne sensors, ground-based sensors (including observations from forces in the battlefield), and sea-based sensors. Looking out twenty years, the US and China militaries could know the location of one another, what they are doing, and how their actions signal the intention to go to war. Both nations will become increasingly able to know the when, where, and how.

One outcome could be mutual transparency. Imagine what AI capabilities will be capable of doing in 20 years. Will the seas be transparent? Possibly. Will preemption be attractive because assurances of its success will be high? Yes. With the prospect of successful preemption available, will opposing forces have their finger on the trigger, watching each other, ready to preempt if they sense the enemy is about to launch? I hope not. Moreover, what if problems exist with one another's AI algorithms? Would the mistake trigger a preemptive strike? And moments later, would it trigger opposing forces to counter the enemy first strike? Aspects of such developments could facilitate significant arms control measures within two decades, or certainly increase tensions. For example, successful AI applications rely on large data set, which will increase dramatically with space satellites associated with communications and observation. This suggests the possibility of an arms control treaty to constrain the development and employment of anti-satellite attacks.

Words Matter

Comments by US government officials on China usually have not been limited to intellectual property and human rights. Often they are expansive and lead the American public and world to believe that China is a rising nation which must be tamed because it poses a threat to the United States. Recently such comments have been made by Secretary of State Pompeo, former acting Secretary of Defense Shanahan, and FBI Director Wray. Many Americans do not read these comments, but rest assured that the Chinese do. The more the aggressive we are, the more the door closes on an open relationship that could increase trust and collaboration. And, the more the Chinese will spend on their military and ways to confront the United States. Obviously, we are building military capabilities intended to specifically take on China. As we do, we will continue to strengthen our capabilities—the military-industrial complex is alive and well—resulting in efforts by the Chinese to resist with larger capabilities in the future than we can field. Surely, in looking out to 2039 that likelihood is momentous. The American people may become the losers.

Any dramatic slowdown that casts doubt on the ability of Beijing to improve living standards could undermine stability and the hold of the Communist Party on power, making it unable to exercise its authority, even with increasingly centralized power and aggressive social control to retain stability. The United States and China will face important issues within the next two decades, including demographic changes that will increase longevity and lower birth rates but reduce the ratio of workers to retirees. By 2039, China will have 100 million fewer workers. In comparison, the US population is rooted in a tradition of immigration and will not fall prey to the same changes. But similar trends fuel concerns over the cost of Social Security and the debt. Many Chinese will be urban, because of megacities and disparities in wealth.

While many developments suggest good times ahead for China, like the United States, they will be accompanied by cultural, political, and social changes. By 2039, will the dynamic between the nations be primarily competitive or cooperative?

Competitive Paradox

Are the United States and China destined to be competitors, and will the competition slip toward military confrontation and conflict? Neither nation has said so directly. But important groups in both nations believe in that destiny. The economic and military rise of China, particularly in the past decade, contributed to the rationale for this forecast to great power rivalry. More recently, the Chinese economy has provided the capabilities to militarily confront the United States and compete for resources and power. Over the next two decades, competition for both economic and strategic influence will intensify a slide toward an eventual armed conflict.

In July 2019 China issued a white paper, *China's National Defense in the New Era,* in both Chinese and

English.[3] Unlike China's previous defense white papers, the new one focused on military reorganization, UN peacekeeping, a moderate rise in budget (and included a commentary on the rise in US military budget), the importance of cyber and space, concern with Taiwan, reiterating its policy of no first use of nuclear weapons and military forces. It has a section on "protecting China's overseas interests," a discussion of China's participation in regional security cooperation (with Russia, Kazakhstan, Kyrgyzstan, Uzbekistan) and China's participation in ASEAN, the Shangri-La Dialogue, and the Jakarta International Defense Dialogue. While it accuses the United States of seeking hegemony, it suggests the Asia-Pacific security situation remains generally stable.

To many Americans, China seeks to push the United States out of the areas it dominates, from emerging technology to global markets. This builds an assumption that conflict is certain, and that it is imperative to win the economic competition and prepare to prevail militarily in the hope of either delaying the inevitable or deterring catastrophic implications of an armed conflict. It is essentially a policy route that offers a pathway back to another Cold War.

Although the United States and China worked together to mitigate the fallout from the global recession, it roused their paranoia. It intensified deep concern in both nations. In China, the fear of political fragmentation emerged from failure to stem the growing disparity in wealth between rural and urban populations. In the United States, because of surging debt, the recession threatened future generations who would be faced with a life worse than their parents. With these emotional issues at play, it was tempting for politicians in both nations to promote conflict scenarios in a quest for power.

Telecommunications and the Internet

Beijing opened Internet service to the general public in 1995, proclaiming "The Year of the Internet." There were some strings. The government asserted its control, mandating that all Internet connections be channeled through international ports established and maintained by the government. In 1997, the government criminalized Internet postings it believed could harm national security. In September 2000, restrictions required Internet service providers to assure the information sent out adhered to the law and that the names and IP addresses were recorded. New constraints continued. But the government began to see the Internet as offering new powers. Party leaders started to increasingly use of the Internet to spread guidance to the public.

Over the past two decades, Beijing has shifted toward an Internet that constricts uses in its favor. The strength of the CPC's control over the Internet rests above all on its commitment to prevent information containing values that it believes are dangerous from spreading among the Chinese public. And it has a "cyber army" to help it, probably about 2 million "Internet public opinion analysts."

Constructive Engagement

Doom and gloom predictions of an inevitable war are dangerous, vacuous, and simply wrong. They stem from the Cold War and are rapidly diminishing in validity. They undermine American pragmatism and inject self-fulfillment in their prophecies. The fears of competition are exaggerated and ignore the progress in globalization and its relevancy. They tend to either overlook or discount structural changes derived from globalization, which have made zero sum notions of international relations essentially counterproductive.

The future will depend on far more sophisticated information technology and new and different global communication networks. Development of text translation tools is accelerating, and by 2028 it is unlikely that foreign languages will inhibit communications, which means an expansion in Internet commerce and close-knit globalization as well as enabling social networking to facilitate increased media freedom.

The future is never surprise-free, and prudence dictates never losing sight of the impossibility of accurate predictions of what will come. There are two ways of hedging against unpredictability. One is attempting to impose a model of economic and international relations based on experience and prepare for the worst outcome: an inevitable conflict. The other involves adopting the genuine American model that combines exploration and experimentation with the promise of what can be done. The latter model begins with an assumption that things can and should be better in the future. These approaches are particularly suited to the future US–China relationship. For most of the next decade, the quest for stable, mutually beneficial relations will rest primarily with the United States because of the economic and military disparities that currently exist. To avoid a path leading back to yet another Cold War, a mutually acceptable collaborative pathway must be developed.

Budgets

The structure of economic relations between the United States and China changed because the production and supply of high-tech goods has become geographically disaggregated and globalized. This is especially true in the case of integrated circuits: the microchips that act as the brains of electronic devices and the central nervous systems of modern telecommunications. Integrated circuits drive computer networks that operate in cyberspace and underpin the economy. Other areas of collaboration include the environmental threat from coal in energy production and energy efficiency. Both nations have supported bilateral agreements on conducting research and development on solar and wind power, capturing and storing carbon gas, mandating cleaner coal production, and promoting alternative fuels for automobiles. Although these initiatives are worth pursuing, American and Chinese companies should expand collaboration in telecommunications, not only because it is mutually profitable, but also because the more immediate connection the stronger the options to thwart the destiny of conflict will become.

Military-to-Military Relations

China could match the United States in military prowess by 2030 in the South China Sea and Pacific if it decided to do so over the rest of the next decade. Its annual military budget toward the end of that decade could easily reach the equivalent of $800 billion (in constant 2019 dollars). Because of the huge stakes, costs, and risks to China, the Chinese leadership has not opted for that course of action.[4]

Let's begin with the issue raised annually by the United States: the lack of transparency on how much and where the Chinese are investing in their military and the lack of transparency on "intent." In fact, the debate over transparency is essentially political, not military. The US military is focused on the military capabilities of other nations, and the Pentagon's interest in what other nations are spending is much less important than gaining knowledge of what potential opponents have, how they operate, how they train, and what they intend to do.

The lack of transparency regarding the Chinese military budget has more impact on the political debate within the United States than it does on military planning or operations. It has become largely a political rationale for protectionism, energy policy, subsidies, and electoral strategies, fueled by the argument that the Chinese intentionally hide their military expenditures to gain political and military leverage over us. The Chinese lack of transparency may not pose an intrinsic military threat, but it can have the important political effect of orienting the United States toward distrust and competition and less toward cooperation. This dilemma could be avoided by forming a joint group of experts on military expenditures like the statisticians of the China–US Joint Commission on Commerce and Trade. The group stemmed from differences between the two nations in measuring trade deficits. Although it never resolved the differences, it helped explain the reason that the United States and China kept coming up with different numbers and allay suspicions on their respective motivations.[5] A similar group of defense budget experts, if put together, would form a transparency commission and achieve results.

Why are efforts not focused to obtain transparency where it counts: on military capabilities rather than expenditures on them? If that becomes the question, more interaction is the best way to gain more insight on Chinese military capabilities, strategy, and planning. Experience in such interactions with other nations suggests how it can be done without jeopardizing national security. In fact, increased interaction provides the opportunity to reduce competition and suspicion, and will likely increase willingness to collaborate in pursuit of common goals.

Joint Experimentation

As both the United States and China move away from depending on militaries that were shaped in the Industrial Age, the value of forces incorporating advances in information technology increases. Not only is the technology changing fast, it accelerates the rates of change in doctrine, force structure, and operational art. This requires experimentation that is basically different from demonstrations and exercises. The latter revolve around how militaries do things today, and militaries tend to present what they are doing now as successful. They frown on mistakes and surprises. Therefore, exercises and demonstrations are interesting for the purpose of deterrence and transparency. Experiments, on the other hand, concentrate on finding solutions. Mistakes and surprises are valuable in helping find solutions that are not only different and new, but better. Many experiments, and experimenters, can generate higher value out of the process by sharing information. Of course, that provides the foundation for research and development as well as the accelerated rate of scientific discovery in all fields. To militaries seeking transformation on the order of a classic revolution in military affairs, sharing the results of experiments is the best and fastest way to succeed with the least risk of surprise.

If the United States and China see each other as enemies, we will be condemned to the waste, danger, and cost of a new arms race. If we accept collaboration to deal with mutual problems such as terrorism and humanitarian crises, joint experimentation might provide the best means of dealing with it. Understanding our respective military forces could become a prime area for joint experimentation.

Cyberspace

While attacks in cyberspace are not responsible for killing people directly, they can tragically disrupt and destroy things our people need: such as electrical power grids, industrial control systems, and communications which could result in collateral deaths. No framework exists within which to discuss ways of dealing with cyberattacks. They are not readily subject to the international law of armed conflict or the arms control agreements of the Cold War. Nor is the concept of deterrence easily applied to cyberattacks because of problems in quickly and accurately identifying attackers. But large-scale strategic attacks, intended to be highly disruptive and destructive at a national level, are different from the kind of attacks that have occurred to date. That is, at the high end of cyberattack potential, the analogy to strategic attacks relationships in the late twentieth century becomes stronger. The likelihood of identifying attackers would rise dramatically and unprecedented retaliation, perhaps including the use of nuclear weapons, could become the only means of striking back. This raises issues on the utility of working with China and other nations to devise an agreed-upon framework for dealing with cyberattacks and exploring the possibility of committing to a "no first use of cyberattack." This could also initiate collaboration on the development of quantum means and other approaches to defending against massive attacks.

Sea Lanes

In 2005, Admiral (Ret.) Michael Mullen, then Chairman of the Joint Chiefs of Staff, suggested in meetings with Chinese officials that it would take a thousand ships to protect the sea lanes, eliminate piracy, reduce terrorism, and constrain the movement of weapons of mass destruction. China acknowledged a common interest in these threats. Discussions have led to what the US Navy calls the Global Maritime Partnership Initiative (GMPI). The overall concept includes the kind of measures that should be discussed with the Chinese as part of the drive toward collaboration in the US–China relationship. But not everyone agrees. Americans who see the future of US–China relations as essentially competitive are troubled by collaboration that opens channels of intelligence operations against US maritime power and diplomatic leverage in those areas where national policies differ. Similar arguments exist in the PLA based on perceived potential efforts against the PLA Navy, attempts to embarrass China by demonstrating the edge of American naval power, or operational control over Chinese forces in cooperative undertakings.

Such arguments are overblown by both sides, partly because of the way the GMPI was structured. It started by assuming that established maritime nations like the United States and emerging maritime nations like China shared common interests in the effort to curb piracy; guarantee access to sea lanes; and prevent surreptitious activities involving weapons of mass destruction, human trafficking, illegal immigration, and drug smuggling. Overall, it took for granted that maritime nations find great individual value in maintaining the seas as a global common and realizing the chances for doing so are better by working in concert. It was intended to be essentially voluntary and facilitate public and private efforts with platforms, people, and protocols. But it was an extremely important initiative that has great promise and could be a model for many other areas of cooperation between our countries.

The GMPI could develop ship-based, aerial, and land-based sensors that ranged from simple radars to sophisticated methods of detecting illicit activities and voluntarily sharing the resulting information. GMPI proponents see it as a step toward expanding cooperation in other areas. These might include disaster relief, fishing and extraction of other ocean and seabed resources, maritime safety, oceanography, hydrography, port and container security, ship construction, weather and sea forecasting, and climate research. However, none of these advances would come automatically or without controversy because vested interests would prefer to maintain the status quo. And taken together, these areas of potential collaboration may not be sufficient to overcome suspicions and distrust that fuel fears and competition. There is truth in what Admiral (Ret.) Dennis C. Blair, the former Commander of Pacific Command, portrayed as the value of the habit of cooperation: The more you cooperate, the more you value cooperation and expand into new areas.

The Uses of Space

In January 2007, the Chinese used a rocket booster intended to launch medium-range ballistic missiles to position an unmanned maneuverable vehicle in low-earth polar orbit. The launch was timed to reach a weather satellite put in space eight years earlier. The timing was precise enough for ground-based radars to guide the vehicle to the satellite in a demonstration of the hit-to-kill, anti-satellite capability proven by the United States in 1985. The Chinese success in hitting the satellite produced a cloud of debris, much of which will orbit the poles for a decade. The destruction of a reconnaissance satellite by a US Navy destroyer occurred about one year later. Had the United States and China begun a sensor-based arms race in space? Not yet.

The United States would respond to an attack on military space-based assets as an attack on the nation that would not necessarily be limited to the space-based assets of the attacker. However, keeping things in perspective, the concern over a conflict in space is nothing new. When the United States and the Soviet Union had developed anti-satellite weapons, they reached a modus vivendi. Both nations recognized the importance of knowing what the other was doing, and for the other to know that fact. We recognized that situation by agreeing not to attack national technical means, a term for satellites that verified compliance with the Strategic Arms Limitation Treaties. In addition, from the outset of the space age, the military uses of space for observation, navigation, and communications have been successful without weaponizing space. Over the past few decades space-based assets became integral to globalization and space became the twenty-first century commons. This stimulated interest in a code of conduct for space as well as a "collaborative global information umbrella," a concept that the United States and China could initiate and open to the entire world.

It is possible that treaty negotiations could be held on the military use of space. Both China and Russia have stated an interest in doing so. Beijing proposed a treaty on the prevention of a space-based arms race. A better approach would be found in the Incidents at Sea Agreement, an agreement that established rules of the road. A code of conduct for space could dodge the issue of what constitutes a weapon in space. For instance, do maneuverable surveillance satellites qualify because they can theoretically collide with satellites or crash into targets on the surface? Instead, it should deal with behavior. It could develop caution or safety zones around satellites, provide notification measures, and restrict actions that produce dangerous debris. As an executive agreement, it would have the legal standing of a treaty and yet be simpler to negotiate under the auspices of the United Nations. This is the traditional solution to managing access to and maintenance of "commons." It could represent an early step back from the precipice of competition for control of space and a step toward collaboration that would benefit the commons in space, which is available to all of humankind.

Global Information

Can a global information umbrella be provided through collaboration with China? Two decades ago, I suggested that the United States could in the future offer global transparency for a conventional armed conflict, its preparations, and its results as well as its aftermath. Since then, technology has improved and the ability to collect information from sensors and process, integrate, and understand data are better. Moreover, China will match it within a decade.

The notion of sharing has increased. A decade ago, few people thought of monitoring the seas in a common way like international airspace. Several web-based virtual crisis centers have emerged in the past decade to provide both satellite imaging and near-real time updates on natural disasters. In brief, a growing network of public and private information centers exists to deal with various contingencies. Working in concert, the United States and China could eventually gather and analyze the data collected from satellites, aircraft, unmanned aerial vehicles, ships, and ground sensors to accelerate transparency. To accomplish this would require a willingness to share more (but not all) of what is gleaned from classified sources and methods. But many of these reservations are holdovers from an earlier age. While we do not want others to know everything, the benefits of openness would be greater than imposing secrecy.

One fundamental assumption of warfare is that opponents never fully understand the where, what, and how of conflicts, known as the fog of war. Artificial intelligence, big data, computer power, new sensors, and quantum computing are lifting that fog. Both the United States and China understand this development and are seeking the means to cloak, hide, and camouflage their forces. But over the next two decades, the chances to discover where an opponent is located, what it is attempting to do, and what it can do are increasing. At some point between stealth and transparency the latter may win, not so much out of perfect knowledge but enough to consider preemption. This is a dangerous phenomenon.

Understanding the Chinese

The single most important factor in the future of US–China relations is developing mutual understanding. That does not mean accepting Chinese policies and actions that conflict with our own or that go against the grain of democracy, human rights, and governance. But understanding is the foundation for maintaining productive interactions. A great disparity still exists between what China knows about the United States, on one hand, and what the United States knows about China, on the other. In large part, this is the consequence of the relative openness of American society. But one is struck by the way Beijing diligently follows congressional hearings on China, articles published in our military journals about China, and the activities of governmental and nongovernmental organizations relating to China.

Chinese secrecy only represents part of the reason why US analysts know little about China. The number of Americans who can speak Chinese is increasing with some 58,000 students taking courses in Chinese language at American colleges and universities in 2007, up by about 50% from 2003. But compared to the US 825,000 students who took Spanish classes in 2007, it seems very minimal. While the number of Americans visiting China has grown dramatically, the number of Americans enrolled in Chinese language and area studies has not.

More importantly, a concerted effort is needed to form the basis of a better understanding of the Chinese. That understanding is analogous to the events of 1957 and American reaction to the Soviet launch of Sputnik into orbit. Amid expressions of shock, accusations of a missile gap, and displays of public hand wringing, President Eisenhower proposed, and Congress endorsed, a broad educational effort to reassert US leadership in science and reassess US national security in a rapidly evolving world. This response was embodied in the National Defense Education Act and the surge of support for higher education that was focused mainly on the university and postgraduate levels. It ranked with the G.I. Bill of 1944 in terms of providing access to higher education.

Today, an effort is required to dramatically expand our understanding of the Information Age, the course of globalization driving it, and the way in which China and other nations are responding. The social and cultural changes in China in the past two decades make cross-cultural assessments increasingly demanding. At present, US–China relations are emerging as a major national security issue and will continue to be for some time. A national effort is needed in order to understand what is essential for us and our children to successfully deal with the Information Age.

Taiwan

The most important security issue affecting the United States and China relationship is Taiwan. Americans have accepted the "One China" Policy—there is one China and Taiwan is part of China—as the peaceful solution to this issue, i.e., coming together peacefully. While many diplomatic communications have been exchanged between Washington and Beijing, and many misunderstandings exist, the underlying policy remains unchanged. And the United States continues military sales to Taiwan because of a long-standing congressional resolution, not a binding treaty obligation. At one time, arms transfers and the presence of the US military within the region may have provided adequate defense for Taiwan in the event of an attack by China, but those days are long gone. Beijing has continually maintained that if Taipei declares independence, China will respond militarily. In fact, given the military imbalance, there is little doubt that China could overtake Taiwan by force in ten days. Little can be done through US presence or military sales. So, the efficacy or importance of arms sales, especially of high technology systems, has little real effect on the military outcome, other than symbolic signaling. It is most important for Americans to stand for democracy, a free press, an effective system of justice and human rights, but every effort should be made to facilitate the peaceful coming together of China and Taiwan and the welfare of our Taiwanese friends. To reiterate, it is not helpful to sell advanced weaponry to Taiwan. In many instances, it has been facilitated by both the Kuomintang (KMT) and the Democratic Progressive Parties in Taiwan for one to appear stronger than the other.

Washington plays into this game that caters to our own military-industrial complex, which leads to sales of the most modern F-16 fighters and modern air defense systems, all of which causes doubt in Beijing about the US commitment to "One China." Although Congress established in law the requirement for the arms transfers, I strongly oppose providing the most modern systems in our inventory. The military-industrial complex should not be enriched by this situation. Supplying advanced weapons to Taiwan is creating a dilemma that is enormously detrimental to all the parties concerned. A way must be found to remove this thorn from US–China relations and every effort made to find a solution for the Taiwanese and Chinese peoples, and for Americans. This will be discussed further in our macro policy recommendations in Chapter 4.

How Much Defense Spending Is Enough

One should begin any discussion of the amount invested in national defense with the commitment to a strong, capable, modern military for the United States. Given the interests of politicians, lobbyists, and journalists, it is difficult to know what that means. Some people assume the more spent on the military, the more capable the military. That hypothesis is wrong. A properly organized and congressionally approved military might look quite different from the current one. Most people pay little attention to this possibility and instead bicker about the latest policy debate in Congress or a banal issue in the Pentagon. It is questionable whether the Department of Defense is organized to bring artificial intelligence, machine learning, robotics, and quantum computers to the table for the US Armed Forces to perform their missions in the world today. One must ask why jointness does not prevail when it comes to installations, transportation, health care, personnel management, and contracting. In fact, each of those enablers remains within the purview of the services, and civilian and military leaders are unable to pursue to emerging requirements because of legislation that is disputably 20 years behind the times.

Looking to the future, defense budgets will become even more challenging. Those who have thought at length about the issues raised in this book think that because of the quickly increasing debt structure, the US will be pressed in a struggle to pay off interest on the national debt (well over 110% debt of GDP). Today, that interest amounts to roughly $500 billion in a federal budget of about $3.3 trillion and GDP of about $20 trillion. But as you look at the likely growth of the deficit, and the unwillingness by Congress to address it, that interest will grow from $500 billion to $1.2 trillion in the next 10 to 15 years. That will total one-third of the federal budget. The natural impulse will be doing whatever is required with discretionary funds. Defense spending is discretionary and making further reductions may be possibly criminal, even if the Pentagon had been re-organized around a new world requirement. It is likely that given our current growth rate, the military budget could be capped at $500 billion sometime in the next 10 years. Our people should be made aware of what is happening. This is very serious, it is serious for our national security, and it is serious for every American, especially our children who will be asked to carry this burden, possibly with a military less funded than we could ever have imagined.

As for decisions on warfighting, they are taken by the Unified Commanders in the field who are directly responsible to the president, but various capabilities that support them are provided by the four armed services and defense agencies, organizations that do not cooperate effectively enough to quickly respond with the best solution. The Goldwater–Nichols Act, which was passed more than three decades ago, sought to redress this, but its intent has never been fully implemented. Even though very well-meaning people head the Pentagon, they are driven by statutory responsibilities, the 80-year-old "Title 10 legislation" and often are unable to undertake across-the-board innovative changes. For example, when troops are committed on the ground, air support comes from the Army, Navy, Marine Corps, and Air Force, and there is NO modern aircraft solely designed and built for air support of our ground forces. The employment of the best air support is simply impossible with the different capabilities, communication systems, and battlefield tactics of the four services and agencies.

As stated earlier, because of our deficit and other competing domestic priorities, defense budgets will be even more challenging. Our leaders should be aware of what is happening in this inevitable vice. And we must remember that the Chinese equivalent military budget could be much larger. This world will look much different in 2039 than it does today.

NOTES

1. Remarks by Secretary Mattis on the "National Defense Strategy," January19, 2018; https://www.defense.gov/ Newsroom/Transcripts/Transcript/Article/1420042/ remarks-by-secretary-mattis-on-the-national-defense-strategy/.

2. Federation of American Scientists; The State Council Information Office; "China's National Defense in 2004;" https://fas.org/nuke/guide/china/doctrine/natdef2004. html.

3. The State Council the People's Republic of China; "Full Text: China's National Defense in the New Era;" http:// english.www.gov.cn/archive/whitepaper/201907/24/ content_WS5d3941ddc6d08408f502283d.html.

4. The Chinese government reports expenditure information annually. In March 2019, China announced a yearly budget of 1.19 trillion yuan ($177.5 billion), marking a 7.5 percent increase from the 2018 budget of 1.11 trillion yuan ($167.4 billion). This follows a recent trend that has seen yearly percent increases in spending fall to single digits. See ChinaPower; "What Does China Really Spend on Its Military?;" https://chinapower.csis.org/ military-spending/.

5. Department of Commerce; "U.S.-China Joint Commission on Commerce and Trade (JCCT);" https://2014-2017.commerce.gov/tags/us-china-joint-commission-commerce-and-trade-jcct.html.

CHAPTER 4

INTO THE FUTURE: POLICY RECOMMENDATIONS FOR A NEW ROAD AHEAD

Over the past several years, I have devoted considerable attention to discussions in China, India, Pakistan, Singapore, and the United States focused on likely prospects of US–China relations over the next few decades. I have come to realize that the experience of the Cold War offers little understanding of the current US–China relationship. I served most of my military career during the Cold War. The strategic framework of the Cold War embraced containment for a half century, that is, the division of the world into a first world including the United States and other democracies, a second world comprised of the Soviet Union, Eastern Europe, and China, and the third world, the African and other developing nations. None of this pertains to today or the future. And China is NOT the new Soviet Union nor likely to become that in the future. It is much different and the long term much more significant.

One of the most complete discussions I have had over the past 10 years has been through what came to be called the Sanya Initiative between five retired four-star generals and admirals from the United States and a similar group from the People's Liberation Army. How to prevent a war between the United States and China emerged as a primary issue among these participants. Initially in the early years of the meeting, the discussions tended to iterate official doctrine of the two governments, but by the fifth year of the discussions they shifted toward ideas that rested outside the official postures and began to explore ideas that were more diverse, new, and collaborative.

During this time, I've come to believe that there is a profound dichotomy in the way that two nations think and plan regarding each other. The US government, particularly the current government, focuses on the near-term relationship between the two nations. It speaks of immediate trade wars, Chinese military actions, intellectual property theft, and cyber hacking, arguing that China is not adhering to the current world order. The Chinese tend to think in terms of the intermediate and long-term futures, and how they hope to shape that future. Xi Jinping speaks of what the PLA "will be" in 2050 and of a Belt and Road Initiative that will be the most important economic development of the entire twenty-first century. American scholars seem to focus on Chinese history and only the immediate next few years.

Understanding this, a few very bright and informed colleagues and I decided to try to forecast the longer-range future of the US–China relationship and to offer about a dozen substantive macro policy recommendations for consideration of the reader and hopefully, eventually, the US government.

In the first three chapters I have attempted to describe what is happening in China and to a lesser extent in the United States over the next 20 years. There have been many arguments and discussions about all of this. However, I believe that, as stated in a previous chapter, China will be the leading country in the world in several areas: gross national product, buying power, military budget (should they choose to apply a world standard of about 3% of GNP to the military), and in several other areas mentioned in this book. China is likely to be a peer in many areas of technology, including artificial intelligence, quantum computing, machine learning, and robotics. And China could well lead in many areas such as telecoms technology, high-speed rail, and commercial nuclear reactors. I personally believe essentially all of that is close to a given.

The recommendations below are provided with all of that as a background, and with the fact that the Chinese have indeed planned for the long term, and that we must indeed look to a future which will be very different than our past. I plea with the reader to understand that I write this book with my thoughts totally devoted to our country and to our children. I write it with the fear that unless we *become real* about an almost certain future, we will significantly reduce the chances of our children to lead their best possible lives in peace and prosperity. And with the great hope that the United States will continue as a bastion of freedom, good intentions, great education, innovation, and a welcoming home for those choosing our country as their own.

It is in that spirit that conversations over the past year from many sources have convinced me that we need a group of very well thought out macro policies that can be implemented by our government to develop true trust and cooperation between China and the United States. This does not mean that we will not compete. But it does mean that we will compete in the spirit of friends, two friends who have the ability to set a pattern for the world and the world's institutions, which will allow future generations to live better lives in peace and prosperity. This world would also set an example for all the other countries of the world to be driven by the United States and China to thoughtful solutions for its great problems, those of pollution, poverty, terrorism, cybercrime, and a continued threat of military confrontation.

It's my belief that we don't have many years to turn the corner on the distrust between the two countries and rely on our leadership to find the way to a better future. These recommendations are meant to be constructive for our leaders' consideration in achieving this future.

Over the past year, the individuals listed in the Acknowledgments and I debated, discussed, sometimes argued, often returning to the discussions of potential areas of interaction and cooperation that could emerge over the next two decades to build cooperation and avoid war between the United States and China. The following list outlines the "winners" from our year of discussions. It portrays initial collaboration that could build the chances of more controversial cooperative issues.

POTENTIAL AREAS OF INTERACTION/ COOPERATION

Northeast Asia Security Organization
China–US Free Trade Agreement
No First Use of Cyberattack
A New Approach to Taiwan
People-to-People Program Driven By the Chinese Premier and US Vice President
Mutual Development Approach to Air and Water Pollution

Collaboration in Quantum Computing, AI, Robotics, and Biometrics
The New Mutual Assured Destruction/Information Umbrella
No First Attack on Space Assets
Tactical/Strategic Nuclear Weapons and Long-Range Strategic Nuclear/Nonnuclear Ballistic Missile Delivery Systems
A Memorandum of Understanding Between China and the United States to Work as Partners to Resolve Nation-States Issues That Are a Challenge to Humanity
South China Sea "Antarctica Rules"

Northeast Asia Security Organization

Over the past decades there have been many incidents that could have risen into something much more substantive, a true confrontation between China and the United States. Without listing all of these, a few examples would be the P3 incident, the Diaoyu/Senkaku Islands, the emerging challenges between Vietnam and China and between the Philippines and China, the challenges of free trade in the South China Sea, the challenges of freedom of navigation in the Taiwan straits, a whole variety of challenges in fishing rights, and oil and natural gas drilling in contested areas.

Today there is no standing organization to address these many possible challenges that might erupt in the future. In 20 years the United States will be second to China in many areas, and these potential conflicts could quickly flame into full-born kinetic warfare. It is a vacuum in world organizations that there are none to directly address the complex issues that will inevitably arise in this critical area of the world. There are examples of such organizations in other regions in the world, such as the OSCE in Europe.[1]

It is my strong recommendation that we coordinate with China and countries and allies in the region to establish the Northeast Asia Security Organization. The structure of this should involve representatives from the major nations of the region. This would, at least at the beginning, include the United States, China, Russia, Japan, and South Korea. It should be a standing organization in an agreed location with significant civilian and military representatives. It would be at least, initially, a forum for discussion and possible airing of grievances and discussion of solutions. In the future, given the great importance of this region, there could be other very important, more formal agreements established. Given the uncertainty of the next 20 years, it is imperative that this initiative be studied and implemented early in the next decade. My experience in the region tells me that there is a genuine thirst for this organization which could develop into much more in the years to come and be a major factor for peace and stability of the region.

China–US Free Trade Agreement

Over the years the United States and China have gone through many different phases of trade. After World War II with Mao and the Communists then in power, there was very little trade at all. And then came the WTO with President Bill Clinton and the opening of world trade to China. Recognizing China as a developing nation was of great benefit to that country in becoming what it is today, a significant, substantial world power. Then came the complications of intellectual property theft, the lack of a meaningful judicial system in China to enforce copyrights or patents and the general misunderstanding of each other's systems to the extent that there was a huge amount of distrust built between the two countries. While we won't forget their intellectual property theft and inefficient enforcement, China has now developed a basic patent and copyright regime and an enforcement mechanism that is now making a difference in international acceptance. This is to the Chinese credit. There has never been such a system or systems for the enforcement of these patent and copyright rights in the country. Today there are thousands of Chinese companies that have copyrights and patents and need to protect that intellectual property. So, as we have learned many times, China is not the same now as it was 10 years ago in so many ways. In the face of all of this is the inevitable growth of China and the prominence of China on the world stage, in 20 years leads to being the number one country in GDP and in many ways, in influence.

It is a mistake to continue to drive a trade policy that causes significant angst, uncertainty, and anger on both sides, and is upsetting the long-term relationship and balance between the two countries in a way that may take decades to recover, while disrupting world trade in general. So thinking over a period of several years, a negotiation should begin with a bilateral free trade agreement that would address intellectual property violations, reduced (to zero) tariffs between the two countries, and mutual respect for each other's rule of law.

When the free trade agreement is enacted this would change the trade relationships with the world in multiple ways and could be incorporated into a "new WTO" concept that would set the world on a long-term, more prosperous journey. For those of us in the United States who are nationalists, over time the United States would be a beneficiary to this agreement. This requires vision, partnership between our two countries, and enormous courage, remembering that there will be many wounded intellects and egos, and that only all the people of our countries will be the beneficiaries. I believe this would be one of the greatest contributions we could make to the benefit of our children and the future.

Currently, roughly $4.5 trillion is traded annually in Northeast Asia, representing more than 60% of the overall regional trade. Today, Asia is becoming like Europe and North America: a system in which members have more to do with each other than with nations in other regions of the world. Asia decoupling is great news for China, but less so for the United States. The American share of international trade will fall below that of other regions. On the one hand, this change reflects the fact that the United States does not need the rest of the world for its survival. In geopolitics that is fortunate but in geo-economics it means we are more dispensable than we think. Indeed, the most significant trade relations for China are with other Asian nations, followed by Europe, and then America in third place.

No First Use of Cyberattack

A no first use of cyberattack agreement could be negotiated to pave the way for addressing rising concern of global cyberattack. The difference with no first use of nuclear weapons is identifying the source of an attack. While proliferation and possible theft of a nuclear weapon has made identifying the state or nonstate actors responsible for launching it more difficult than identifying the source of cyberattack, the growing concern over this could promote joint China–US efforts to swiftly and accurately identify the source of a cyberattack.

A decade ago, security experts viewed malware as the chief danger to computer networks. They believed malicious software codes including the viruses, worms, and Trojan horses used by hackers to infect computers and networks that linked them together were the central threat. Today, however, the security environment is changing. Dangerous vulnerabilities have been revealed in the past decade, but they stimulated major advancements that offer protection. Malware attacks possess inherent weaknesses. Even though viruses can jump from machine to machine (hence the prominence of distributed denial of service attacks and data theft), all the devices attacked can be immunized against them and swept clean. The basic problems are tough: can an attack be detected in time to stop or limit its effects, can damage be minimized, and can the functions and processes disrupted by an attack be quickly restored? Over the past 10 years, the answer to those questions has become yes. Malware attacks are essentially a nuisance, but they are not a threat.

Security threats exist when rogue hardware (or microchips) with malicious logic are inserted during design, manufacture, shipment, or installation of devices. With few exceptions, the process involves companies located in multiple nations. Probably all microchips found in the United States contain inputs from China and, correspondingly, almost all microchips found in China have inputs from companies located in the United States. Rogue hardware could exist in microchips that play vital roles in the networks, computers, and electronic devices of both nations. However, if they do, current means of detecting them leave much to be desired. The US and Chinese economies, along with most other nations, risk undetected rogue hardware. That has resulted from globalization over the past decade. Meanwhile, security experts have become less concerned about rogue hardware because firms based in the United States produced the microchips. Those firms had vested interests in detecting malicious logic under rigorous security procedures. Both government and commercial purchases could trust the supply chain to provide electronic equipment and components, which run almost everything from coffee makers to electrical grids and telecommunications.

At present, trust in hardware is shaky. Whether the design is American, Chinese, European, Indian, Iranian, Japanese, Korean, or Russian, the manufacturing is globalized. Most complex digital systems use many third-party blocks. Designs rely heavily on computer-aided programs, tools that may themselves be configured to insert malicious code into systems. In going through the various stages of development, portions of a design are stored on many different platforms and repeatedly exchanged among firms. For example, an American maker might combine designs from different branches of the company with designs from third-party vendors in Europe, India, and the United States, and fabricate the microchips in a Chinese factory. Although these global networks provide savings in cost and afford higher efficiency, they make security more complicated.

Global manufacturing poses essentially the same threat to both the United States and China. Either nation might corrupt the process in ways that endanger the other, and third parties can attack both. Is there a greater risk to the US? Not really, although the publicity given to vulnerabilities of critical infrastructure in the United States suggests higher danger. Reliance on the Internet and telecommunications—the dynamos of growth—in Chinese megacities will negate substantive differences between the United States and China. While both nations have launched broadband expansion programs in rural areas, the Chinese effort dwarfs that of the United States. China relies on reversing the disparity in wealth between urban and rural areas and uses the Internet for this purpose as well as an instrument of population control.

Therefore, collaborative efforts to increase trust in global production are natural. They should take place to furnish microchip designs that incorporate tests against rogue hardware and techniques for detecting malicious logic, building on the promising work by the Defense Advanced Research Projects Agency and Chinese agencies. And they should encompass demonstrations and promotion of greater transparency in microchip design and the devices that utilize them.

The preceding paragraphs have discussed the challenges of the modern cyber world. That world continues to change, and with the advent of artificial intelligence and deep penetrating tools both for the delivery of, and prevention of cyberattack, we face a very uncertain future. One which is fraught with potentially huge devastation to our societies. With the ability to "take down" a nation's total economy in the form of its Internet structures (and thereby its economic viability), power grids, and smart data centers and technologies through cyberattack, it should be top of mind for our country to address this threat with determination and certainty. As we move into a world of quantum computing and security, it will not get better. And this is a challenge which the Chinese face equally. It is an area where today we are globally devoid of rules and understandings.

As we look at the United States and China over the next 20 years, we believe it is of the greatest importance that we address this challenge. I believe that could take the form of a no first use of cyberattack commitment by both countries. This has not been the norm for American foreign policy, but this is not a future based on norms! If the United States and China took this unprecedented step, it is certain that many nations would follow There would be great pressure for them to do so and joint pressure of the two largest countries in the world on the rogue states to do the same. I acknowledge that this would take substantial understanding and verification. And deliberation on the details will take months or years. The joint presence of experts on both sides to ascertain the critical indicators and to be in a position to verify will be enormously important to such an understanding. But the effort here is without question worth the time and deliberation. No first use of cyberattack should be one of our major initiatives between our two great nations.

A New Approach to Taiwan

Taiwan is the most important single issue standing between a future of peace and cooperation between China and the United States. The Chinese have, over many decades, attempted to establish undisputed boundaries around their country, boundaries that are fully recognized as a part of greater China and internationally accepted by other countries in the world. We should note that in general, they have not been imperialistic in their hundreds of years of history. The Chinese believe that Taiwan is a part of greater China, and the United States maintains that the "One China Policy" is our position as well. The United States has made it clear that our full intent is to bring together this China/Taiwan "oneness" only by peaceful measures. Many decades ago, the United States Congress put in place a resolution that the United States would foster the certainty of a "peaceful coming together" through arms sales from the United States. While this has been a topic of continual disagreement between China and the United States, it continues and many in China believe that it is evidence that the United States is truly not supporting a "One China Policy." My position on arms sales was covered earlier in the book, and I won't further that discussion here. But it is my belief that with the support of the United States, in whatever way we can engage with both China and Taiwan, that a peaceful resolution to a "One China" is possible. My belief is that given the Chinese are somewhat flexible in the terms of such an agreement to bring the two countries together with no disagreement, I believe that with United States support for such a peaceful resolution, the Chinese might be very giving in terms of providing assurances for the long-term well-being of the Taiwanese people. This might include a continuance of the present democracy, essentially a hands-off policy except for any suggestion of a separatist movement, and a strengthening of mutual ties for the betterment of the economy of Taiwan. While no one can know exactly what those terms might be, I believe strongly that this could be for the overall best long-term interest of the Taiwanese people and for stability in the region regarding China. So the Policy of the United States should be strongly articulated to play a supportive role in this development, to encourage China to leave a free democracy and Western standards in a semi-autonomous Taiwan, and to curve our arms sales of the most modern US equipment. If we were to look at the world 20 years from now, this Policy would be beneficial to not only the US–China relationship and the Taiwanese people but also to the world. Of course, the United States should work with our allies and friends in the Pacific as we pursue this policy. But again, the significance of the issue warrants a new direction to resolve the Taiwan question peacefully. This must be at the TOP of the United States government policy for the long term!

People-to-People Program Driven by the Chinese Premier and US Vice President

People-to-people programs are some of the most important initiatives between our countries. As a matter of Policy we should undertake a major initiative at the very highest level: the vice president and the premier of China. The programs should encompass all areas of engagement to include military-to-military programs, economists, universities and students, business, and tourism. Failure to genuinely bring our peoples together will lead to growing suspicion, lack of trust, and a growing likelihood of mistaken assumptions regarding each other's national goals. My involvement in Asia has convinced me personally that our friends and allies in the region would strongly support this initiative and would become an important part of it.

There should be strong encouragement for military-to-military engagement at all levels. This should be from the level of the Central Military Commission in China to the Joint Chiefs of Staff of the United States. It should eventually include all levels of military-to-military engagement. The United States could propose that cadets and midshipmen from the military academies could be exchanged, not just for a few weeks, but for the full curriculum. It should be noted that over the decades, we have done this for many countries of the world, including South American nations and others. The eventual trust between our militaries will be a key factor in the overall stability of our relationship and will be a strong antidote to the potential Thucydides Trap described by Graham Allison.

Many will take exception to such game-changing recommendations. I ask the reader to reflect on the 20-year future, and what action we should take in 2019 to preclude the worst outcome for our children.

In the area of education, there is much to be done. Today there are more than 300,000 Chinese students in our universities. We have only about one-tenth that number of Americans in Chinese universities. The exchange of views between professors and staff of all disciplines will be another critical area of engagement. And in business-to-business relationships much more cooperation and research should be undertaken.

Mutual Development Approach to Air and Water Pollution

To truly reduce global carbon emissions, our two nations—the two most polluting nations—must cooperate if we are to make any progress on the major solutions. Whether one believes that human beings are causing the change in weather or whether it is the change of nature, it is clear that we will be much better off if we have a clean environment in which to live. This specific Policy initiative might be under an Established Govt-to-Govt entity, perhaps a subgroup of the above-mentioned Vice President/Premier Initiative and should include university research, the establishment of cooperative programs, and the understanding of technologies to reduce carbon emissions meaningfully. This effort should also include other areas of global pollution such as plastics in the ocean.

For those who have not followed the huge challenge of ocean dumping, it needs much greater attention. Should you go to many of the ports of the world, you would see the dramatic challenges of trash, petroleum, and plastic in our oceans. A visit to such ports as Karachi would be a memory you won't forget. The trash and plastics of the Indian Ocean have drifted into the shores of such ports and in many instances must be plowed out in order for a ship to come into port. This ocean dumping is killing our fish, our coral reefs, and our oceans. Solutions exist, but without the United States and China in the leadership, are unlikely to have a meaningful effect on our globe.

Collaboration in Quantum Computing, AI, Robotics, and Biometrics

Intense pressure will be imposed on the US–China relationship over potential and challenges and opportunities for cooperation in these scientific fields. One challenge to policymakers involves managing stress in this field to preserve space for working together when it serves both American and Chinese interests. In 2017, China unveiled a national plan to reap the benefits of artificial intelligence: the New Generation AI Development Plan. The goal is to become a global AI leader by 2030. General Secretary Xi reinforced those objectives in a speech to the 19th Communist Party Congress in 2017 and with a politburo study session later that year. Today, the US probably leads in the investigation of these emerging sciences and in their use. But the lead is narrowing. China is likely to catch up and possibly surpass the US in some of these areas. So logically, both nations could advance faster in the efforts to better understand and use these scientific fields if we worked together.

Both the United States and China understand that the future of solutions for medical problems, medical scanning, new drugs, and medical care in general lie in these new sciences. We also know that these new areas of technology really are our future in terms of the development of our economies and the shift from a strongly manufacturing world into something that is much more efficient and productive. Importantly, these areas are also the future of military capability. Those of us who have spent a lot of time in China know that the Chinese understand all of this very well. And they are applying tens of billions of dollars annually to the development of these technologies. It would be most important for our companies, for our universities, for our joint research, for the betterment of our children's lives, and for national security that we settle together on how we can effectively cooperate in the use of these sciences for improving the world around us. In the context of the people-to-people programs, an earlier recommendation, this sub-engagement should be undertaken on the basis of improving our world but not to interfere with our critical security programs and must be undertaken in a most determined manner.

The New Mutual Assured Destruction/Information Umbrella

A phenomenon I want to highlight in this book is the growing capability of transparency of a very large "battlefield" (including space, air, ground, and oceans). This phenomenon more and more is that both the United States and China will have the ability to make every battlefield transparent. That may happen in 10 years or 20 years, but it will be before 2039.

Today the US no longer has a monopoly on the dominant understanding of very large battle arenas. We lead in the race for achieving transparency, and China has entered it. Both nations will have the ability to make large battle arenas transparent. That is, an ability to understand where the forces of both contenders are, what they are doing, and what they could do. The technologies come mostly from commercial developments of AI, advanced sensors, robotics, machine learning, and quantum computing to make my dreams of 1995 seem quite sleepy in the future.

The geographic area is now considerably larger and includes the oceans and space. The United States is hard at work continuing to develop that "system of systems," and the technologies coming from commercial development of AI, advanced sensors, robotics, machine learning, and quantum computing are coming together. That assembly of military knowledge of the battle arena will change the "fog of war," perhaps leading to taking the first step to initiate conflict before the opponent does. This is strategic in every way, and all of us who have done war planning fully appreciate what this means. The desire to strike first may be sometimes irresistible. This is both a remarkable capability and hugely dangerous.

In the case of the United States and China, as a matter of Policy, it is my strong suggestion that our Departments of Defense and State start talks about this new world of a new "mutual assured destruction," transparency, and deterrence before we are face-to-face with the capability. Of course, this is not an area in which we would share huge amounts of data and technology. But we should recognize that this is our future and that of China. The technology that makes preemption attractive in military affairs will emerge as a global danger. The sooner we and China begin to deal with this emerging danger and start to reduce the implications of military transparency, the better. Knowing the peaceful use of this technology for counterterrorism, humanitarian disasters, and the greater good of mankind needs to be balanced in the domain of military affairs. It will be a challenging task. We and China will have to deal with implications of the growing concept of preemption for the sake of both ourselves and the world.

One of the areas in which we might cooperate is in the area of gradually starting to share limited knowledge of what each side knows of the other's capabilities. This will obviously be very sensitive for both sides, but we should always keep in mind the longer-term goal of trying to find a way forward with each other for a peaceful and nonkinetic future. In this regard, working together to develop an understanding on both sides of the other's capabilities could result in a desire to find ways to avoid the great dangers of the ultimate transparency of the battlefield and the desire to hold our own technology close in the belief that it is superior to that of the other nation. And to the danger of a leadership structure that may not be fully cognizant of the results of the conflict.

We might begin with some limited exchanges of information shared from various sources: space, electronic intercepts, AI, new quantum computing, and which would protect our individual national security. These insights would be helpful to starting a process of trusted dialogue toward a solution different from exchange of fire. This, of course, is very challenging, and no one is thinking about it today, but I am confident that in this period of 20 years this will become a pressing discussion one way or the other, and that we should see the future and do something about it before it is too late.

At some point in the future, given the assumption that TRUST between our countries will grow, and given the dramatically increasing recognition of abilities to identify potential preemptive actions, the US should propose daily exchanges of its sensor-based data on Chinese forces in the South China Sea in exchange for similar sensor data on US forces from the Chinese. The data on locations, activities, and tracks would be provided for each other's locations and movements; China to provide the locations and activities it has on US forces and the US to provide similar data on what it believes are the locations and activities of PLA.

No First Attack on Space Assets

Classical concepts of war from Sun-tzu to Clausewitz to today's military leaders emphasize to hide forces and obtain accurate and timely information about their opponent. Clausewitz argued that accurate, essential, and timely information was always going to be limited by the "fog of war." He may have been correct. But over the next 20 years, the fog has a good chance of dissipating, driven by space-based observation and communications. Today the US holds the edge. But China is narrowing the gap. China's space program has a complex structure, built on organizations in the military, political, defense-industrial, and commercial sectors. The PLA historically has managed China's space program, and it continues to invest in improving China's capabilities. Both China and the US have demonstrated the ability to attack satellites, and while both nations have not demonstrated the use of nuclear and other forms of radiation to sever the flows of information to and from satellites, both nations could probably do it. But the idea of an agreement to not launch the first attack on an opponent's space systems becomes less important as the redundancy of the number of satellites grows. In short, the military benefit from the number of an opponent's space-based systems makes it increasingly difficult to get vital military value from a first attack, because the opponent could and probably would attack the initial aggressor's space assets. Theoretically, the danger of first attack could be reduced by agreement that their satellites would not be stationed in areas of space far enough in distance that moving closer to other satellites to suggest they were preparing to attack the opponent's satellites. Initial launch of land-based missiles (ground – and aircraft-launched anti-satellite weapons) could not reach all the satellites.

The critical nature of all these national strategic space assets warrants that we undertake a Policy to discuss a Treaty to avoid the great danger of either an actual or a perceived first attack on the other country's assets! There would be little doubt in the future that an attack by one nation on any one or more of these critical satellites would be seen as an act of war. The risk of miscalculation is enormous as hundreds of space vehicles are put into orbit, each of these being a critical element of a nation's capability. To this end, it would be stabilizing and beneficial to both China and to the United States to have a no first attack on space assets agreement as a part of our portfolio of moving together as peaceful nations into an uncertain future.

Tactical/Strategic Nuclear Weapons and Long-Range Strategic Nuclear/Nonnuclear Ballistic Missile Delivery Systems

Many of us thought 20 years ago, thanks to many efforts of world leaders such as Senator Samuel Nunn Jr. and Senator Richard Lugar in the United States, that we had started to see the beginning of the end of nuclear weapons. With the collapse of the Soviet Union, two events bolstered that hope. One was the INF Treaty, formally "The Treaty Between the United States of America and the Union of Soviet Socialist Republics on the Elimination of Their Intermediate-Range and Shorter-Range Missiles" signed in 1987. The other took place in the 1990s as Russia pulled out its tactical nuclear weapons (not covered by the INF Treaty) from areas that had left the Soviet Union. At the time the major US concern was that some of these weapons might be transferred (or sold) to groups seeking them. (At the time, I proposed an agreement between the US and Russia to stockpile these tactical weapons outside both nations, in a desolate and guarded location. It was not welcomed.)

Most had hoped that we would certainly find a way to limit these by all countries, especially come to grips with the fact that only a few would have them, and that the rest would be controlled. That world is no longer the world in which we live. And we have seen the proliferation now of the threat not only from the "nuclear countries" that the world community has somehow accepted: India, Pakistan, France, the UK, China, Russia, Israel, and the US. Now there are other nations, with the growth of technology and irresponsible cross-border-sharing of this terrible destructive technology. This group today is North Korea and Iran, but in the future may spread to other nuclear terrorist threats and nation states.

To complicate the issue of strategic nuclear weapons, we see the growing importance of tactical ballistic missile-launched nuclear weapons and other delivery methods for tactical nuclear weapons, each designed by different nations for different purposes. The INF and Strategic treaties of only a few years ago seem to be coming apart as we see growing Russian interest in tactical intermediate-range nuclear missiles and with the United States moving to ensure that our strategic nuclear forces are modernized, and that the US nuclear weapon inventory is renewed. (See Fig. 10.)

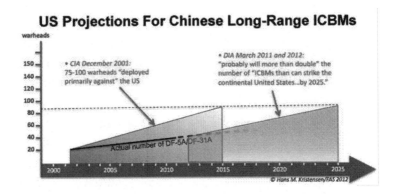

Figure 10

And today, we are confronted by a new world of "tactical nonnuclear ballistic missiles and delivery systems," which some might call strategic nonnuclear ballistic missiles. An example in the US is the growing importance of the Army's ATACMS system, an example of such a very high-quality, high-technology nonnuclear capability. The obvious advantage of short time of flight and therefore greater likelihood of accurate target kill against a moving target has become a factor in the growth of these tactical ballistic missiles. The Chinese see the PLA Strategic Missile Force to be of the greatest importance as they look at defending the seas surrounding China as well as an immediate offensive capability against the threat of a Taiwanese declaration of independence from China. (As mentioned earlier in this book, there is no more important strategic initiative for China nor a more important Chinese–US issue to be resolved than the Taiwanese one). It is in this context that the Chinese have built hundreds of very reliable and capable tactical ballistic missiles designed for the attack on Taiwan and/or the Eastern and South China Seas. In the face of this, consideration for long-term cooperation between the United States and China to resolve the nuclear weapon issues, as well as the ballistic missile and long-range delivery systems issues, seem to us to not be likely for the 20-year near term. There are simply too many factors, some tactical and many strategic, dealing with both of these critical issues.

Nevertheless, in the spirit of this book, we should not shelve these issues. The United States and China as the world's largest and second largest countries will have huge power and influence to start, to regulate, and to apply pressure to other nations about each of these issues. To have any degree of resolution, however, will require considerable discussion, *TRUST*, and understanding, and is likely to not happen in the context of the existing dialog structures.

We believe that the beginning of this trust and this process could be as a new "element" of a United Nations Charter somewhat re-formed around the existence of the two great nations leading the world responsibility together. It could take a form of the UN Security Council with the five major decision makers involved and with the opportunity for all nations to be included both in the arrangements and in the acceptance of new standards and regulations that could lead to definitive arms agreements.

A Memorandum of Understanding Between China and the United States to Work as Partners to Resolve Nation-States Issues That Are a Challenge to Humanity

Much of the discussion of relationships between the United States and China often focuses on competition between the two nations. Part of this focus is the past associated in economics and war, which form the basis of a competition for wealth, power, and dominant prestige.

But the times will be different in 20 years, and we need to gaze into that future to look at how we can establish a resolve between the two great countries of the world. Without that partnership, we will inevitably wind up on opposite sides, and everyone loses. Today one only needs to view the two challenges of North Korea and Iran. In each, we have inevitably wound up on the opposite side from one to another, thereby prolonging the danger to the world of dictators and situations that threaten our people and the world around us. This partnership requires years of TRUST building and development of cooperation between our militaries and our policymakers. Many will say that this is simply impossible and represents the words of a dreamer, that their view and ours are radically disposed to always be on opposite sides.

But I have seen much of the decision-making and have come to know many of these leaders who would quickly step up to be involved in discussions that could lead to that eventual partnership. We've seen this in the fight against piracy, we've seen it in many other areas with the United States and China, and we have not exhausted our imaginations to make it work. I think we can! It will take years, and patience, and many elements of trust building such as the initiatives we have outlined in this book. The point is that in North Korea the Chinese have been dealing with this in their own way for decades, and a situation developed that is not completely satisfactory for the Chinese national interest.

So it is with the United States that many attempts have been made on our own. We established agreements, built around threats, and these resulted in very little substantive direction or purpose to reach a final solution. It is obvious to me that the Chinese know a lot more about North Korea than we do. They have a 1,000-mile border with North Korea, there is a significant amount of trade across that border, and the peoples of northeastern China intermingle in many ways with the people of North Korea. The Chinese over the years have learned vast amounts of the North Koreans' capability and continued developments, including those around the advancement of nuclear weapons and military systems. That knowledge goes far beyond what is possessed by the United States.

Today, our interests are somewhat aligned. The Chinese do not want a nuclear state on their border, and we don't want a North Korea that is armed with nuclear weapons that may be able to reach America, Japan, and other nations throughout the Pacific. They want a stable North Korea, separate from a growing prosperous South Korea. The United States is not totally in line with that vision. We both need to eat our pride and work together as partners to develop solutions for North Korea. These could include, for example, a formidable agreement to de-nucle-arize North Korea, with guarantees from the United States of the nuclear umbrella over South Korea and Japan and from China for North Korea. A multinational inspection team could be led by the Chinese with the United States having complete access for verification. There could be an agreement for a peace treaty relatively quickly between the United States and North Korea, including economic sup-port from both the United States and China for North Korea to develop into a booming economy like the one we've seen come out of their neighbor to the south. None of this will happen without the cooperation between the United States and China. And we will never find a com-plete solution without our two nations working together and with their respective friends, the Russians, the South Koreans, and the Japanese to reach ultimate peace and sta-bility. Foreign policy is not just for one nation with regard to all others. It should morph into a new world where the two most powerful nations are working for the peace all of us so dearly desire, especially in the most troubled areas.

Neither China nor the United States wants Iran to become a nuclear weapons state. And we would prefer India and Pakistan to be rid of their nuclear weapons. Over the next two decades there is a growing global possibility of a new nuclear weapons race among "regional nations." For instance, North Korea nuclear weapons could generate nuclear forces in Japan and South Korea. Iran's efforts to develop nuclear weapons to counter Israel's nuclear weap-ons could trigger a nuclear response from Saudi Arabia. Vietnam could perhaps be seeking to obtain nuclear weap-ons to counter China. Turkey could become involved. NATO could be very different by 2039 (if it still exists).

Together we just might reduce the inventories of nuclear weapons, and perhaps abolish nuclear weapons entirely.

Suppose China and the US worked together to prevent all other nations from owning and developing nuclear weapons. It would be similar to the early concept of the United Nations Security Council acting together to prevent other nations from waging war. The concept could involve the elimination of intermediate-range nuclear weapons on the part of China, Russia, and the United States and eliminating all the nuclear forces of Great Britain, France, India, Pakistan, North Korea, and Israel, and preventing Iran, Saudi Arabia, Japan, South Korea, and any other nation from developing or obtaining nuclear weapons. Also, Russia, China, and the US would reduce their nuclear weapons, possibly ultimately to zero. In effect, this would conform to the recent Treaty on the Prohibition on Nuclear Weapons.[2]

South China Sea "Antarctica Rules"

There are some interesting parallels between the South China Sea and the Antarctica Treaty (December 1959) and its Madrid Protocol (1998). In the treaty, there was an agreement of the nations that had claimed areas of the Antarctica to not assert their claims. No military forces were allowed on land, and nuclear weapons and radiation material from nuclear weapons development were not allowed. While the treaty applied to the land and ice shelf and not ships, in the Madrid Protocol treaty nations must inform ship movements and purposes. The Protocol restricts "mining" (oil drilling at sea), and wildlife (fishing) cannot be harmfully interfered with without a permit. It also limits discharge of waste from ships. China is a member of the Treaty and Protocol.

The Treaty and Protocol could be a guide to an agreement on the South China Sea to not assert claims of territory, other than maritime limits and boundaries recognized as the low-water line along the coast, the territorial sea (12 nautical miles), contiguous zone (24 nautical miles), and an Exclusive Economic Zone (200 nautical miles, plus maritime boundaries). Chinese Premier Li Keqiang said at the Bangkok summit meeting November, 2019 of the Association of Southeast Asian Nations (ASEAN) that China was "willing to work with ASEAN, under the consensus that had been reached, to sustain long term peace and stability in the South China Sea, according to the timetable set for three years" to agree to a South China Sea code of conduct, due for completion within three years.[3] (See Fig. 11.)

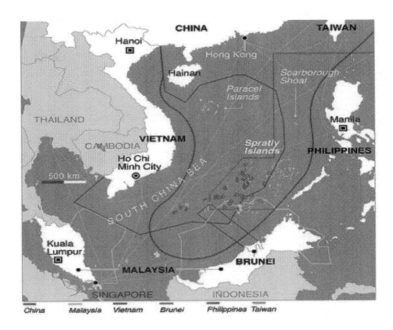

Figure 11

CONCLUSION

This book has been an attempt to look at the future of China and America in 2039. As the book suggests, the United States doesn't do futures very well! But the Chinese do them quite well now and have done the same over the past thousand years. The book has offered some insight into what the Chinese and American systems will look like in 20 years: what the economies will appear to be, what the national security policies will be, and what the relationship between the two countries might be. Then we should ask ourselves what Policies might we have undertaken in 2019 and 2020 to optimize the US position and mutual cooperation with the Chinese, avoiding something like what turned out to be the Cold War with the Soviet Union and avoiding the Thucydides Trap. We have reminded ourselves that China is very different from what the Soviet Union was. This is a people and an economy that are destined to be the number one economic player in the world. We need to realize that, and to find ways that we can benefit America and the world from our relationship with them. We start from the fact that these are people who were our strong allies against the Japanese in World War II, and they are a people who have, in all of their history, had very little interest in being an imperialist nation. They are also a nation that I believe has a desire to be a cooperative partner with the United States. As Graham Allison points out, the Thucydides Trap presents a very staunch challenge for the two great nations in the world to reach this kind of understanding.

Given the differences between the systems in terms of goals and rules, it is not surprising that we talk past each other and miss the full intent and significance of what is said. We come from backgrounds that are different. And as such, we differ in interactions with one another on the governmental and commercial levels. Americans have come to expect immediate communication on all levels to develop relations and mutual understanding. The Chinese are dedicated to delivering what the hierarchy expects.

There are two sides of this story. In dealing with the Chinese, I became aware of a factor that influences Americans but often is not realized. It originates from the fact that we believe we almost always have the complete story, the factual news, and the insights on issues not only in our own country, but also internationally. But we frequently see only our own side of the story and do not realize how the facts are viewed from other perspectives. This realization is significant and opened my mind to the need to internalize the story from the other side before making up our minds. I have found this realization to be especially true in the case of the Chinese. The government and public have views on issues such as North Korea, the South China Sea, Taiwan, and others. But it is important to get the real beliefs, the real story from the Chinese. Often those views are not blotted by Communist ideology or other factors but reveal their true thinking on the most important issues. If we listen attentively and understand them with respect, I am convinced that we can find solutions. If we do not want to listen to their views, the likelihood of true solutions is reduced. During the Sanya Initiative, we attempted on two or three occasions to have Americans explain the Chinese side of the story to the Chinese and for the Chinese to explain the US view of the story. This resulted in considerably better understanding of how common solutions might be found.

The contrast between Americans and Chinese was illustrated by an event on Capitol Hill when five visiting

Chinese generals and five American generals of the Sanya Initiative met with several US senators and representatives. After two of the senators discussed relations with China, the meeting turned to international affairs. As the senators talked about alliances, one of the Chinese generals interjected that it would be good to address the meaning of alliances. To paraphrase, he began by remarking: "We are not like you. We have no alliances and never had them. It is not that we are against you. Our tradition is not to interfere in sovereign nations if possible." The ensuing exchange was instructive for all of us present. The meeting also discussed the single-party system in Communist China. One of the PLA generals observed that it appeared strange that the United States was opposed to the single ruling party in China yet had been supportive of the single-party system in Japan for about 60 years. "What was the difference?" he asked.

There are deep differences between the United States and China. A very important difference was brought to light for me by my old friend, Li Lu, who explains that the Chinese system is built around a political meritocracy and our United States system is built around an economic meritocracy. Hence, in China the leadership of senior government and Party organizations is conducted by people who have proven themselves in many different positions from the city level to province to national. Through that process they have developed a deep understanding of how their government works. For example, when a new initiative is required, such as the development of artificial intelligence or quantum computing, the national government can provide guidance, the local governments will follow, and financing and resources are provided to ensure the success of the initiative.

We have seen this process at work in many instances such as the control over the monetary system, huge infrastructure development, and their approach to building relationships. Their approach is different! The meritocracy in China is a political hierarchy that defines merit as knowledge of socialism with Chinese characteristics and skill in applying that knowledge. The central role in assessing merit is assuring that individuals with higher authority support the proposal or action and are effective in their leadership. In order to become the governor of a province or the president of the country one must navigate through the bureaucracy to satisfy the people one works for, as well as the rules of the hierarchy. Today, that Chinese meritocracy involves 90 million Communist Party members. The Chinese meritocracy is complicated, and Americans must be careful in assuming they can reach agreements quickly.

Frustrations among Americans often develop because of the lack of relatively quick response to proposals. We expect frequent emails, phone calls, and dialogue to reach an agreement, alternative, or disagreement. The Chinese are less prone to be engaged on a day-to-day basis. But that does not mean they do not care about the matter at hand. In communicating with Americans, the meritocracy requires that they gain the approval of their superiors. Policy changes are slow in coming. While tending to assume knowledge of Chinese diplomacy, governance, and business, our understanding often is based on Western reporting and analysis that fails to grasp Chinese thinking on a given issue. This presumption can lead to a serious flaw in our relations. We must be sure of our understanding of the Chinese—not just talking points—including the rules of their meritocracy.

Li Lu argues that the American system is built around an economic meritocracy where those who have produced the greatest companies, the greatest products, and the greatest innovations have been the core of the huge success, growth, and stability of the United States. Of course, I would add to this, *the great blessing that our founders gave us* in establishing the form of government that allows our economic meritocracy to flourish, our system of justice, our Constitution, our freedoms, and our great institutions. All of this has laid the basis for our meritocracy to function well, even though government officials in many instances may not have the range of experience that our counterparts in China may have.

My attempt is to remind everyone that while our country will remain exceptional in so many ways, it is extremely unlikely that we will continue to be the largest economy in the world by either total GDP or buying power, but it raises the hope that we can stay the shining light of righteousness, innovation, justice, and freedom, and that we can remain an international military player, coexisting in an understood partnership with the Chinese military.

It is my belief that proceeding as we are today, the relationship between our two great countries is very likely to be a drift toward an outcome that none of us wants to see. We are headed toward a new form of military confrontation, one that we would not recognize today. And again, we must realize that China is not the Soviet Union and that past experience is mostly irrelevant in looking at that kind of conflict. Containment is not an option. The outcome of that kind of relationship is not likely to be easily resolved and could not be in favor of the United States.

In this book primarily in the areas of national security and national security-related economics, I offer several major policy directions with some specificity that might be taken *over the years* ahead to put our countries into a TRUST built, strategic partnership, in a new world order for the great benefit of all of our people.

As we listen to media locked in the drone of daily events, I fear we have spent far too little time addressing the future. To not consider the future, to not be realistic about its facts, to not tell the truth about what it will be to ourselves and to our people, is to put that future in grave danger. To not develop and implement the future directions and policies that will preserve all that we stand for is a great failure of leadership. As we listen to our leaders today, it's not apparent that future-oriented policies are being addressed. We do not understand the culture of each other, either the United States or China, and we certainly don't understand the true positions of both sides, side by side. We hear the United States position or in China the Chinese position, but we rarely understand each other's positions. And in almost no case do we ever achieve any level of the most important word, TRUST!

To give thought and bring new policies to this, at a very high level in America, in government, academia, and in the broad American panorama is of enormous importance.

NOTES

1. The OSCE (Organization for Security and Co-operation in Europe) has a comprehensive approach to security that encompasses politico-military, economic and environmental, and human aspects. It therefore addresses a wide range of security-related concerns, including arms control, confidence – and security-building measures, human rights, national minorities,

democratization, policing strategies, counterterrorism, and economic and environmental activities. All 57 participating States enjoy equal status, and decisions are taken by consensus on a politically but not legally binding basis.

2. Nuclear Threat Initiative; "Treaty on the Prohibition of Nuclear Weapons (TPNW);" https://www.nti.org/learn/treaties-and-regimes/treaty-on-the-prohibition-of-nuclear-weapons/.

3. Soe Zeya Tun, "China says ready to work with ASEAN for South China Sea peace," *MSN News*, November 3, 2019, https://www.msn.com/g00/en-ph/news/world/china-says-ready-to-work-with-asean-for-south-china-sea-peace/ar-AAJLg2h?i10c.ua=1&i10c.encReferrer=aHR0cHM6Ly9zZWFyY2gueWFob28uY29tLw%3d%3d&i10c.dv=15.

ACKNOWLEDGMENTS

I am grateful to a very special group of friends who helped to frame this book during the past year on weekly conference calls. They included Admiral Thomas B. Hayward (Ret.), former Chief of Naval Operations, widely admired and deeply experienced in defense policy; David M. Walker, former Comptroller General of the United States, author, and prominent voice in US policy, as well as a visiting professor at the United States Naval Academy; John A. Knubel, former Chief Financial Officer of the Department of Housing and Urban Development and former staff member for Henry Kissinger; and James R. Blaker, former Deputy Assistant Secretary of Defense. The EastWest Institute and Red Bison with the strong support of my business partner, Martha Bejar, arranged a series of important and informative seminars during the past year that were focused on US–China relations. I have benefited greatly from my friendships over many years with C.H. Tung, the first Chief Executive of Hong Kong after the handover in 1997; Ren Zhengfei, Founder and Chief Executive Officer of Huawei Technologies; several members of the Committee of 100; Fan Gang; Liu He; the Economists 50 organization in China; and many retired American and Chinese generals and admirals who participated in the Sanya Initiative over a

10-year period. I have benefited over the past 20 years from discussions with many very prominent and knowledgeable friends, including Hank Greenberg, Li Lu, Victor Fung, and Ronnie Chan. Zoe Leung of the EastWest Institute was especially helpful. Zoe was invaluable proofreading the manuscript and offered in-depth insights on Chinese history, politics, and economics. Importantly, Sebastian Alfonso, a most accomplished student from Lakeside School in Seattle and president of his senior class, now at Stanford University, participated in this book project for a summer and offered the views of a new generation, which are included in Appendix 3.

Most importantly, my close friend, Jim Blaker, mentioned above, provided the most important discussions and contribution in making this book come to life.

APPENDIX 1

A FORK IN A ROAD, A CHOICE TO COMPETE OR COLLABORATE

We focused on potential interactions that could foretell a stable future if adopted by the United States and China or, if rejected, could signal a descent toward war. Those interactions are listed below in roughly chronological order over two decades. They start with collaboration on international terrorism. Interestingly, my dialogues with PLA interlocutors in the Sanya Initiative pointed to such interactions as pivotal events on which future relations between the United States and China could emerge. Given the limitations on our ability to accurately predict the next twenty years, I have offered two scenarios.

The first, *The Trap*, a term Graham Allison and others use when referring to the Thucydides Trap, named for the Athenian historian of the Peloponnesian War. Allison, like Thucydides many centuries later, argues that when a rising power threatens to displace a ruling hegemon, the resulting stress on the international order results in a violent clash as a rule, not the exception, and it usually turns out to be bad for both protagonists.

The second scenario presents an option of *cooperation*. Embedded in this notion is a growing effort on the part of the United States and China that are likely to remain the most important nations economically and militarily in avoiding conflict and working toward mutually beneficial outcomes.

They illustrate paths that could emerge in the next two decades. The first involves events that could lead to armed conflict, and the second could reduce the chances of going to war. Both look back from 2039. These scenarios are unlikely to be the only ones that will shape the future, but the way the United States and China deal with them is important. How they are resolved will shape issues that arise in the relationship between Washington and Beijing in the next 20 years.

A Competitive/Combative Path: Scenario 1

Commercial relations between the United States and China prior to 2018 had grown enormously for decades to the benefit of both nations, the Asia–Pacific region, and the global economy. Then again, the rest of their relationship had become tense. Washington regarded the economic policies of Beijing as unfair. Moreover, China was building the military forces to challenge the American presence in the region. In response, Washington adopted harsher means of reacting to Beijing that were focused on new tariffs and increased military activity in the South China Sea. The tariffs on Chinese goods responded to the theft of intellectual property and abuse of the open market system. But a more serious concern involved the technological rise and efforts by China to control digital advances such as 5G networks, artificial intelligence, and global infrastructure, under the

"Made in China 2025" project. Beijing perceived the trade war as an attack on its economic structure.

Xi faced the dilemma of accepting an unpopular deal with structural changes that could be mitigated on the margins and enduring economic prosperity or pursuing a nationalistic course that further weakened the economy, fomented social unrest, and eroded the political legitimacy and authority of the Communist Party. At risk was the much-cherished dream that he embraced. He gambled that the economy could weather the trade war and that the United States would acquiesce. Xi also tried to find an accommodation to the dispute without losing face and seeming to bow to US demands.

China retaliated by imposing high tariffs on US agricultural products, automotive products, and other goods. In addition, it ended support for sanctions against North Korea and criticism of North Korean nuclear weapons, and threats of selling volumes of US treasuries and a limitation on rare metals of which China has about 70% control. Meanwhile, the United States maintained tariffs with only minor adjustments and demanded reductions through the American presidential election in 2020. Before then, however, the Chinese had offered free trade agreements to Australia, Cambodia, Indonesia, Japan, Laos, Malaysia, Myanmar, New Zealand, Pakistan, the Philippines, South Korea, Thailand, and Vietnam. By 2022, most of them had agreed to the proposed trade deals.

In retrospect, the Chinese actions added to its declining growth in GDP from 2019 to 2022. The Communist Party dismissed internal criticism by blaming the decline on the American efforts to contain China, which were backed by internal propaganda, and identifying US agents via social media. It altered the 13th Five Year Plan and adjusted the 14th Five Year Plan beginning in 2021 to shift from a market economy and delay reductions in SOE budgets, particularly by those firms that produced world-changing technology and military equipment. Elsewhere, the BRI had taken hold and was generating revenue and trade. The growth in science, technology, engineering, and mathematics (STEM) education announced in 2017 was paying off by 2022 in terms of skilled workers and scientists, particularly given the targets of the 2025 vision. The focus on allegations of US efforts to contain China had some impact on the quality and quantity of returning Chinese citizens, in part because of the American clampdown on visas and concern with the number of Chinese students in enrolled advanced education. In short, private firms in China were meeting most of the demand for innovation.

But the gap between the rich and the lower-middle class was widening and stirring concerns. Criticism was increasing and demonstrations were breaking out. To tamp down the discontent, the leaders of the Communist Party argued that the source of the problem was the United States, which sought to inflict another century of humiliation on China. And the Communist Party was asserting its destiny to make China great again. Beijing remained active in international organizations which included the United Nations, largely to contest American efforts to mobilize nations against China. In addition, the Chinese became one of the major supporters of international collaboration in favor of global warming, in part to challenge the United States for its limited support.

The risks of a confrontation in the South China Sea increased in 2022 when a US submarine ran into a Chinese mine designed to engage ships based on their acoustic signature. The submarine was not lost but was heavily damaged and some of the crew were killed. China assisted in keeping the boat from sinking and being salvaged by the United States. The US Navy increased its freedom of navigation operations in the region and expanded backup force capabilities. In 2024, Chinese GDP growth rate had grown to 7.2%. A few years later, the Philippines announced it accepted an offer to rebuild and refurnish docks and harbor facilities at Subic Bay under the Belt and Road Initiative.

In 2027, China offered lucrative trade agreements to the members of the European Union, which France, Germany, Greece, Italy, and Poland accepted. Surveys conducted by American trade and industrial associations revealed that US companies faced difficulties in obtaining and retaining their Chinese business interests. As a result, many left China, particularly those firms in advanced technologies. The proportion of companies who had moved production or were planning to do so had grown substantially. The Committee on Foreign Investment in the United States was directed to deny investments by Chinese firms and individuals. And one year later, the United States barred Chinese from its colleges and universities, and China reciprocated by expelling Americans from its colleges and universities. Chinese efforts to generate expertise in computing, economics, and artificial intelligence succeeded in producing some five million STEM graduates per year by 2028.

The decline in US–Chinese relations generated both strategic debates and wargaming efforts. Separately, military discussions and wargames addressed three concerns: convincing the opponent not to react militarily, coping with a preemptive attack by the opponent, and launching a successful preemptive attack. Both nations were focused on these potential operations, which reflected gains in military intelligence driven by space-based data, sea-based sensors, and communications intercept and code breaking driven by artificial intelligence and quantum computing.

Both the United States and China began making large investments in their militaries in 2023, particularly space-based communication and sensors, hypersonic weapons, and artificial intelligence that were focused on integrating available data on their opponent. From that time, the United States and China moved away from arms control discussions on the uses of space and cyberspace. China invested more in strategic nuclear and tactical forces. After the mining incident in 2022, the South China Sea became the center of intelligence activities, sensors, and contingency planning. Both nations focused on one another and believed that was where a war might start.

The application of robotics, quantum computing associated with communications, sensors, and artificial intelligence generated extensive debate on preemptive warfare in the US and Chinese militaries. Although they were certainly not going to discuss preemptive warfare, both nations worked from similar preemptive assumptions: the interaction of strategic and tactical preemption. The US and Chinese forces assumed that growing real-time tactical knowledge of one another in the South and East China Seas contributed to dealing with preemptive attacks and counter-preemptive planning. This rising concern assumed that Chinese units were preparing to attack, and that led to reducing military intelligence and communications to signal awareness of a potential attack that would back up diplomatic warnings. It was a dangerous concept. But the PLA capabilities to mount a preemptive attack on US forces was growing. Moreover, the American side added another planning factor: how to indicate the relationship between the two forces was nearing a conflict in a manner that the opponent would not dismiss the warning as simply propaganda.

Although PLA capabilities had expanded its presence globally, its greatest strength remained focused on the near seas. Within that arena, it matched the US military in the precision accuracy, and although lacking in real-time battlefield knowledge of friendly and enemy units, its advantage was growing. But the United States and China did not accurately gauge one another's strength, and instead assumed their own forces were superior. That hubris led to a conflict in 2038. It did not last long, being largely a naval contest limited mostly to the South China Sea. The US Navy destroyed many PLA Navy submarines operating beyond the primary conflict zone, and the Chinese succeeded in destroying many naval and air capabilities deployed by America and Japan in the East China Sea. Both the United States and China used tactical nuclear weapons against opposing naval forces. The conflict did not escalate to the use of strategic nuclear weapons, and relatively little collateral damage to civilians was sustained from conventional and tactical nuclear weapons. Both nations also used cyber weapons that resulted in devastating communications. Their systems operating in space were likewise devastated. Neither side won the two-month conflict.

Despite rival claims of having won the conflict and imposing a truce on their opponent, the damage sustained on both sides was debilitating. China lost most of its naval and air forces, while US naval and air components operating in the South China Sea suffered heavy losses that included roughly half the active inventory of their maritime forces worldwide by the time the truce was announced. Both nations were profoundly changed; their governments collapsed.

Constructive/Cooperative Path: Scenario 2

The focus of discussions by the United States and China centered on their trade relations until late 2019. The stock market gyrated through the first half of 2020 as trade talks moved toward the start of a new world order. As part of the initial agreement, China agreed to lower its tariff rate by 50% and not to challenge a slight US tariff increase.

Avoiding the Trap

Meanwhile reformers in the politburo eliminated restrictions on foreign investment to private enterprises, although national security firms would uphold stiff barriers to foreign investment. The United States reciprocated, allowing Chinese firms and individuals to have more than 50% ownership in most American enterprises, but national security firms were exempted. US disagreements on market access and unfair commercial practices with other trading partners were resolved. Meanwhile, foreign banks were allowed in China. The two decades from 2019 were productive for US/China:

In 2020 the Northeast Asia Security Organization was formed. Beijing joined a five-member deliberative body on international security with Japan, South Korea, Russia, and the United States. Its intention was agreeing to a way of handling military issues in the South and East China Seas, and to generate international support. In 2021, China offered a free trade arrangement with the United States that was accepted. In 2022, the vice president of the United States took on the goal of increasing people-to-people exchanges, including officials from the Departments of Agriculture, Interior, Energy, and Homeland Security; the Environmental Protection Agency; military-to-military points of contact; scientific laboratories; and business executives and board members. China agreed to the exchanges and offered similar participants. In 2022, as a result of a partnership with the US, China, and North Korea and the United States signed an agreement on denuclearization. North Korea and South Korea opened their borders and moved toward peaceful business relationships, and North Korea development and prosperity skyrocketed. In 2023, China reduced its number of state-owned enterprises. Its five-year plan was focused largely on a new Social Security system. The household registration system (hukou) was modified and day care for children introduced in urban areas to permit women to earn the average family income.

The "Made in China 2025" Program: Initiated in 2015 as a ten-year blueprint to create a modern industrial base, it was targeted on about ten strategic industries, namely, next generation information, high-end numerical control and robotics, aerospace and aviation products, maritime engineering and high-tech products, railway equipment, electrical devices, new materials, biomedicine and high-performance medical appliances, and agricultural machinery. By 2025, many of those goals had been achieved and most foreign smart equipment had been replaced including robotics, cloud and big data, new software, information technology, and the security of widespread blockchain implementation.

Military Relations (2022–2039): China proposed a no first use cyberattack agreement in 2022. While the general concept had been discussed between China and the US in various United Nations offices, it had never been of much interest to either nation. It had been informally discussed by the Obama administration and Chinese government representatives in response to cyber espionage and hacking of government data by both nations. The informal discussions could not agree on what each would consider the networks of potential targets that would be prohibited by an agreement. The proposal of working toward an agreement of what a no first use cyberattack would cover was accepted by the United States. The working group proposed the potential targets of a no first use cyberattack would be in the event of an agreement.

The following initiatives were undertaken:

People-to-People Exchanges (2021): China agreed to support the exchanges hosted by the premier and vice president. China agreed to support the efforts of American and Chinese university extensions to both nations with graduate curricula in economics, military affairs, and technology trends. Moreover, both nations would extend visas allowing foreign students with degrees to stay in their nation for five years after obtaining the degrees.

Air and Water Pollution (2025): In contrast to the Trap, in this cooperative scenario, China welcomed chances to work with the US in devising means of reducing carbon dioxide in the atmosphere. Both nations would support joint intellectual property on solar, wind, and nuclear fusion power generation.

Quantum, Biometrics, and Artificial Intelligence (2029): China welcomed close and long-lasting collaboration in research and maintained applications of science into various fields, particularly medicine. Both nations supported joint intellectual property in these areas.

Free Trade (2030): The United States and China reached a free trade agreement after years of discussion that had begun in 2020.

Intellectual Property (2030): In a spirit of collaboration and cooperation, the Chinese dramatically reduced intellectual property theft, becoming one of the top five members of the IP Index.

Cyberattack (2031): The United States and China agreed to no first use of cyberattacks and would work to include additional signatories to the treaty.

Space Observation and Communications (2032): The United States and China agreed to no first use of attack on space observation and communication and worked together to include additional nations in the treaty.

An agreement on no first use of cyberattack was reached in 2034. Meanwhile, discussions on armed forces concluded that the military presence on islands in the South China Sea claimed by China would be reduced. Both nations also agreed to joint basing in the South China Sea to provide humanitarian assistance. The proposal reflected the mutual intent to reduce growing means to preempt attacks by one another. The Chinese agreed to the proposal in 2030.

In 2032, the ruling Kuomintang party in Taiwan accepted the offer to initiate discussions on reunification under the rubric of One China, which subsequently began in 2039. Could this development portend future cooperation between the United States and China? The expansion of this military cooperation led to the further expansion of the Charter of the Northeast Asia Security Organization. In terms of collaborative/cooperation, its original motivation was focused on resolving the risks of confrontation among member nations. But the discussions suggested interactions of military forces within the South and East China Seas could be revised. The Northeast Asia Security Organization became a forum on interaction, including experimentation and deep discussions of preemption. This raised the opportunities of an information umbrella, no first use cyberattacks, no first use attacks on space observation and communication, and basing in the South China Sea.

APPENDIX 2

WHY THE US DEBT CRISIS MATTERS

I'm indebted to my Naval Academy classmate and friend, The Honorable John Knubel, for this valuable piece on our national debt crises, as well as its causes and consequences if we fail to address the reality. I am in agreement with him.

Today, America faces a new, daunting, and unprecedented choice: Revise social insurance programs, allocate a larger share of the gross domestic product to the public sector, accept the risk of a drastic cut in resources dedicated to our national security, or accept continued growth in our debt to unprecedented levels that will threaten our national security and our future.[1] Independent analysis illustrates the reality that if current budget trends continue, US defense spending will drop by more than 20% to less than $600 billion, adjusted for inflation, unless the national public debt is allowed to continue to skyrocket. Especially considering the Pentagon's historical resistance to transformation, at this level of resource availability, it is doubtful that our country could support our current engaged foreign policy with a strong military through 2039.

For our discussion, the debt crisis challenge can be divided into component issues as detailed below.

The Failure of Past Efforts to Control Debt

Past debt control efforts have focused on the absolute value of our public debt measured in dollars. It's easy to understand the public and media focus on this measure because the number is readily available from the Treasury. But it is not the correct metric on which to focus for purposes of understanding the threat's magnitude or for measuring progress when ultimately the country is forced by credit markets to implement a strategy to constructively engage the issues. The metric to use is the debt-to-GDP ratio, not the absolute value of the debt. This public debt-to-GDP ratio metric is used by the International Monetary Fund and the World Bank. This emphasizes the political reality that debt can be allowed to grow, when accompanied by economic growth, *if the growth in debt does not exceed the growth in gross domestic product.*

A Constitutionally Based Solution

History shows us that Congress and the political parties are not capable of controlling their appetite to borrow and spend. We believe a lasting solution will require enactment of a fiscal responsibility amendment to the US Constitution under Article Seven. The amendment needs to be focused on controlling the public debt-to-GDP ratio. Drafts of a sample amendment involving a cap on the public debt-to-GDP ratio, along with sample reduction targets, including recommended adverse consequences for Congress if the targets are missed, have been written. A copy is available upon request.

During the Reagan years, Congress came within one vote of sending a Balanced Budget Amendment to the country for ratification. Since then and because Congress hasn't shown a desire to engage the issue, efforts have been focused on the state-led initiative under Article Seven. This effort should be supported because unless the 34 state applications required for the state-led amendment process are achieved (the current count is 28), Congressional action is unlikely to be triggered before an economic crisis occurs.

Restoring Discipline to the Budget Process

The amendment should demand suspension of pay for Congress if the public debt-to-GDP ratio targets as defined in the amendment above aren't met and/or timely budget and appropriation bills are not passed as part of the annual budget process. We also recommend a capital budget be established so legitimate borrowing is justified to fund multiple-year capital projects that benefit future generations as well as current generations. These can be separated from consumption that benefits the current generation only but passes most of its cost on to future generations. To summarize, a capital budget will separate legitimate borrowing for projects benefiting current and future generations from consumption spending where benefits are exclusively enjoyed by current generations but where costs are passed on to our children. On a general basis, this approach better matches measuring the intergenerational costs and benefits of federal government programs.

Adopting Fair Tax in Lieu of the Income Tax

The exclusive constitutional purpose of taxation is to fully fund federal government operations. Our recommended fair tax would be progressive and imposed on consumption rather than the current system that taxes income and productivity. Our rationale is: Whatever is taxed, the economy produces less, so if consumption rather than income is taxed, both productivity and economic growth will grow faster than they otherwise would, while savings are enhanced, reducing the cost of capital. This taxation regime will therefore better support a growth-oriented "get out of debt" strategy. It is the only politically feasible strategy.

Such a taxation policy would include a national sales or a value-added tax with refundable credit for low-income earners. This system would be more efficient than the current one and would resemble systems used today in the European Union and China. It would encourage people to save, which is not generally an American practice, while reducing the balance of payment deficit that's a concern because a large balance of payment deficits enables the "sale of America."

Past tax cuts have been justified because they will "pay for themselves." The theory is tax cuts stimulate additional growth and therefore pay for themselves while not adding to the deficit. This simply isn't true because after-tax revenue has been historically insufficient to cover growth in spending. The resulting public debt growth is only partially caused by the revenue loss from the tax cuts. It is because of a failure to control spending. A complicating factor is that our spending is currently growing faster than revenue, even without tax cuts, because of the sizable growth in population-driven social insurance programs. In addition, social insurance programs comprise more than 60% of the budget (and rising) and are excluded from the annual Congressional budget process. The trend toward an uncontrolled budget spending pattern has been with us since the Reagan administration when the nation initiated its current "borrow-and-spend" habits. Hence the resulting explosive growth in the public debt and public debt-to-GDP.

The latest Congressional Budget Office projections, published during the summer of 2019, expect spending to rise by about 5% annually 2019–2020 while GDP and revenue increase 2.5% annually. The result is a public debt-to-GDP ratio that's projected to grow from its current level, which is higher than it has been at any time since World War II, to 140% debt-to-GDP at the end of our time horizon. This tests America's creditworthiness and threatens the value of the dollar and its future as the world's primary trading currency.

The Economic Doom Loop

The World Bank and International Monetary Fund (IMF) analysis shows that as the public debt-to-GDP ratio grows, economic growth, revenue, and job creation slow. This can lead to what we call an "Economic Doom Loop" that is already evident in the US data. As the public debt-to-GDP ratio increases, economic growth slows along with revenue. In the absence of spending control, this results in higher public debt-to-GDP ratios, still slower economic and revenue growth, and a downward spiral.

Social Insurance Program Reform

Adjustments are needed to restructure social insurance programs like Social Security, Medicare, and Medicaid so spending growth can be controlled and aligned with projected revenue where revenue projections are based on reasonable economic growth assumptions. In addition to social insurance program changes, reform must include defense and other discretionary spending that makes up less than 40% of the budget compared to more than 80% following World War II. (Significantly, only this portion of the budget comes under the annual budget review process while social insurance programs are driven by formula-related population statistics.) Social insurance program spending can only be controlled by program-authorization-related congressional reform.

Rationalizing Defense and Discretionary Spending

The United States currently fields the strongest military in the world. But this status is threatened as these budget trends continue along with economic growth and job creation. Analysis shows that defense and other discretionary spending will be reduced if the public debt-to-GDP ratio is allowed to continue to grow unacceptably. Current CBO projections support a reality that during the twenty-year period, resources available for national security will shrink by as much as 20% in inflation-adjusted terms. The Pentagon needs to prepare for this internal budget threat. But like the rest of the federal government, the Pentagon bureaucracy has become bloated. The Pentagon's effectiveness is also hampered because under the Goldwater–Nichols Act, reforms that created the CINCS structure, we now thankfully fight as an Army, Navy, and Air Force team but still budget separately. Reforms should include more consolidation, reducing duplication of service capabilities, and other budget rationalization initiatives. Finally, we believe the rest of the federal discretionary budget has grown too large and must be right-sized to address program duplication and reduce the familiar sources of inefficiency: waste, fraud, and abuse.

The Leverage Provided by US Capital Markets

We've discussed the sanction-based power markets: The US enjoys this benefit because the dollar is the world's largest trading currency, and the fact that it still dominates the transaction volume of the Basel Bank for International Settlements. In addition, because the US stock market is the most liquid, largest, and best regulated in the world, we have additional positive influence in our competition with China; that is, influence to supplement ongoing efforts to counter violations of patent rights, limits on market access, and other violations of Fair Trade practices defined by the World Trade Organization (WTO).

More specifically, the largest Chinese companies still rely on access to US markets for capital. Some of those companies produce surveillance equipment, arms components, and other equipment that ultimately supports military threats to the US and our allies and/or hinders our goal of seeing China emerge as a more open and democratic society. Americans are unintentionally financing their development.

We should improve our review of Chinese disclosure compliance with required SEC and related reporting requirements, particularly with respect to those companies that are in the arms development and manufacturing business as well as the production of capabilities to support Chinese persecution of minorities and government surveillance.[2]

During the Cold War with Russia, a great deal of effort was devoted to ensuring we avoided technology transfer to the Russians and supported development of the Russian threat to NATO in other ways. It would be wise to improve a similar capability to do the same in the context of the current competition with China while avoiding referral to the Cold War terminology.

NOTES

1. For a partial list, see Admiral Mike Mullins' statements made while he was Chairman of the Joint Chiefs of Staff: http://the-hill.com/homenews/administration/105301-mullen-reiterates-threat-excessive-debt-poses-to-nation. See also Defense Secretary James Mattis' confirmation hearings and "The Moment of Truth: Report of the National Commission on Fiscal Responsibility and Reform" (Washington, DC: The White House, 2010).

2. For a more comprehensive and eye-opening analysis of these issues, see "Why and How the U.S. Should Stop Financing China's Bad Actors" by Roger W. Robinson, Jr., in *Imprimis* (Hillsdale, MI: Hillsdale College, 2019).

APPENDIX 3

INSIGHTS FROM OUR NEXT GENERATION

During the research for this book, I asked Sebastian Alfonso, a senior in high school and president of his class, to sit in on the weekly discussions of other contributors to the book. A summary of his thoughts is reproduced below.

The media report on China in sweeping generalities, offering little middle ground between China as oppressor and China as global innovator and economic power. Like many others, I am capable of reeling off figures and naming the issues of the day: surveillance state, espionage, the Belt and Road Initiative, "Made in China 2025," and so on. I will be the first to acknowledge wrongdoing on the part of China that is blaringly evident even to me, just as American transgressions must be recognized. As a nation, the United States has shared its values with the world by force if necessary. I am not being overly fatalistic when I claim that we no longer have the luxury. I cannot speak for well-connected American political elites, but China seems separated from my own experience by a sea of cultural difference. It is dangerous to view China only through a lens purely informed by American values.

We tend to underestimate the importance of cultural differences.

Our effort in recent history has been focused on remaining the foremost global innovator in addition to the greatest economic and military power. China is a significant threat that we demonize. It has committed its fair share of wrongdoing, but we must make a concerted effort to work together. Long ago we dismissed mercantilism as a flawed economic theory, yet with China and ordinary Americans our interaction with other nations represents a do-or-die zero-sum game for supremacy. This mentality sets us up for failure and slows down the potential US and Chinese growth.

Around 400 BCE, Thucydides stated that a situation in which an up-and-coming power has supplanted a current superpower necessitates war. We cannot fall into this eponymous trap or risk global catastrophe. The stakes are much higher than economic superiority. I do not claim expertise beyond that gleaned from discourse and research. I am 17 years old and a student at Lakeside School in Seattle. But if one thing is clear, the United States must look forward and change its approach to US–China relations. The current course leads away from progress and collaboration.

As we listen to statements by the president on trade, doubt is cast on the long-term prospects for real improvements in US–China relations.

Sebastian Alfonso

William A. Owens

Admiral William A. Owens is the Executive chairman of Red Bison Advisory Group, a company which identifies opportunities with proven enterprises in China, the Middle East, and the United States, and Red Bison Technology Group which installs and operates high speed networks in large office complexes. He was the long-time Chairman of CenturyLink Telecom, the third largest telecommunications company in the United States. Owens serves on the board of directors at Wipro Technologies and is a director of several private companies. He serves on the non profit boards of EastWest Institute, Seattle University, the Center for Excellence in Education, and several others. He is a member of the Council of Foreign Relations.

Until 2015, Owens was the Chairman and Senior Partner of AEA Investors Asia, in Hong Kong, and Vice Chairman of the NYSE for Asia. Owens served as the Chairman of Eastern Airlines as well as 23 public boards including Daimler, British American Tobacco, Telstra, Nortel Networks, and Polycom.

Owens was the CEO of Nortel, a Fortune 500 Telecoms company, CEO/Chairman of Teledesic LLC, a Bill Gates/Craig McCaw company, was the President of Science Applications International Corporation (SAIC). and served on the boards of the non-for-profit organizations; Fred Hutchinson Cancer Research Center, Carnegie Corporation of New York, Brookings Institution, and RAND Corporation.

Owens is a four-star US Navy veteran. He was Vice Chairman of the Joint Chiefs of Staff, the second-ranking United States military officer. He is widely recognized for bringing commercial high-grade technology into the Department of Defense for military applications. Owens was the architect of the Revolution in Military Affairs (RMA), an advanced systems technology approach to military operations, the most significant change in the system of requirements, budgets and technology for the four armed forces since World War II. He served as Commander of the U.S. Sixth Fleet from 1990 to 1992, which included Operation Desert Storm. Owens also served as the deputy chief of Naval Operations for Resources. Owens was senior military assistant to two Secretaries of Defense (Cheney and Carlucci). He was a nuclear submariner. including tours as Commanding Officer aboard the USS Sam Houston, USS Michigan, and USS City of Corpus Christi.

Owens is a 1962 honor graduate of the United States Naval Academy, has a BA/MA from Oxford University, and an MBA from George Washington University. He has written more than 50 articles on national security and authored the book "High Seas." His book, "Lifting the Fog of War," was published in April 2000 with a revision published in Mandarin in 2009.

Owens has received numerous recognitions and awards: the "Légion d'Honneur" by France, and the highest awards given to foreigners by the countries of Indonesia and Sweden. He was named as one of The 50 Most Powerful People in Networking by Network World, one of the 100 Best Board Members in the United States for 2011 and again in 2016 awarded by NACD, and the Intrepid Salute Award in recognition of his business achievements and support of important philanthropic activities. Owens is active in philanthropy to foster Chinese-American relations including over 10 years of dialogues between the most senior retired officers in the United States and Chinese militaries.

Made in the USA
Monee, IL
24 February 2020